OFFBEAT BALLET

The Interesting Stuff

To Jacqui
I hope you enjoy this and we have more laughs together in the future.

OFFBEAT BALLET

The Interesting Stuff

Written by a surgeon with help from dancers of every sort, plus many other experts – includes a (removable) adult section!

JOHN BENNETT FRCS DCH

BROWN DOG BOOKS

First published 2022

Published under licence by Brown Dog Books and
The Self-Publishing Partnership Ltd, 10b Greenway Farm,
Bath Rd, Wick, nr. Bath BS30 5RL

www.selfpublishingpartnership.co.uk

ISBN printed book: 978-1-83952-524-7
ISBN e-book: 978-1-83952-525-4

Cover design by Kevin Rylands
Internal design by Mac Style

Printed and bound in the UK

This book is printed on FSC® certified paper

MIX
Paper from responsible sources
FSC® C013604

Dedication

To all barmaids and hairdressers, wherever they may be found. Keep up the good work – your worth compared to that of psychiatrists, support groups and advice columns is grossly underestimated.

Biographical Details: John Bennett

Barfly, automobilist, piano player, JB qualified in medicine from the universities of St Andrews and Manchester then trained as a surgeon. Ever the student, he became a BA from the Open University, then MA in Medical Ethics (University of Wales) and took diplomas in Child Health and Medical History. Mindful of his next career, he took to ballroom dancing, which he taught whilst on the surgical faculty of Southern Illinois University. After this he returned to the United Kingdom to work for the National Health Service where he dreamt of life on a cruise liner in the Caribbean selling dances and stories to the rich and shameless.

Acknowledgements

'All art is theft – it is what you do with the loot that counts.'

As the reader embarks on a roller coaster ride through the chapters devoted to anatomy and physiology, the stories of various ballet companies, their venues and artists, it will become plain that this has not all come from research the authors have done on original material and records. Frank plagiarism has never been our intention, but there is a limit to the number of ways a story can be told. Where possible we have acknowledged sources, and we gladly thank the multitude of well-wishers who have willingly given their time to advise and help in a variety of ways.

Disclaimer

Despite rumours to the contrary, this book has not been adopted for the A-level English (or any other syllabus) of any of the current examining boards. Yet.

Contents

Prolegomenon

Ni bydd dofth ni ddarllend.

An inscription high up on the south end of the Free Library, Museum and School of Art (a beautiful building in Cardiff, opened in 1882, it is no longer quite symmetrical as part was demolished to allow the road next to it to be widened; this road is now pedestrianised but the building was not put back). For those of our readers whose Welsh is poor, it may be rendered in English as:

He will not be wise who will not read.

Introduction

For some people the question 'What is ballet?' is somewhat ridiculous – it is their life, their obsession, their way of earning a living. This book will probably not tell them much that they did not already know – but it might! For others, ballet is an evening out – a method of relaxation and being transported away from the trammels of day-to-day life to a magical world of beauty. For yet others it is what is written on the invoice for extra-curricular activities for their children!

This book came out of the collaboration between a ballerina (principal artist and education officer) and a surgeon. An unusual combination, to be sure, but one where the interest of the 'lay person' whose curiosity has led to misconceptions meets the expertise of the professional. There are a lot of things in this world we don't know – and more that we don't know we don't know. But rather than subject oneself to learning in a tedious way – rather like one of the author's experience of Shakespeare (he reads it not so much for enjoyment but in the vain hope that, like taking medicine, 'it might do him some good') – we hope to make the following pages interesting and fun to read – for everybody. Who knows what is going on in the minds of the audience – there are probably as many different things as there are people there. Just what makes a ballet dancer 'tick'?

With this book, find out what JB learnt about ballet, and what some of his ballet advisers learnt about the audience – and have fun.

JB: In a television documentary about The Royal Ballet one dancer complained that she was too tall and had difficulty being matched with a partner. Are dancers getting taller and (like the rest of us) fatter? How heavy is the average ballerina and could I throw one in the air? There have been drunk nurses I have been barely able to stand upright. There must be a spring to start off the lift. How are young boys taught lifting? We are taught injections on oranges – one imagines a dancer starting with a sack of something, then perhaps a dwarf/child, then small ballerina etc.

A: They say an average height for a female dancer is 5′4′ (1.63m). This then means she is able to fit into group work easily and with the average male dancer being generally 5′10′ (1.78m) or over, it means when the girl stands on her pointe shoes and the man is behind her, then her head will come just under his eyeline. This is seen as a good match in an ideal world, but of course you can get smaller men dancers or taller girls for example, which makes the match a little more tricky. However, if these dancers are amazing a company will be reluctant to turn them down unless it was completely impossible for them to be matched. Taller dancers in The Royal Ballet, Zenaida Yanowsky for example, can only be matched with one or two male dancers in the company. If any of her partners become injured and cannot perform, she is forced to wait until they have recovered. In contrast, a smaller dancer could more easily be matched to someone different while her partner recovers.

JB: Partners seem important. I assume your usage of the word is in the old-fashioned sense and not the modern euphemism for a live-in lover! I always dreaded forming up into teams and the like when I was a 'Junior Mixed Infant'. We would all line up against a wall as if facing a firing squad (an apt simile, you might think) and then each team captain would take it in turns to pick someone. You obviously hoped to be chosen early on as that was a sign that you were a better footballer, or 'soldier' if we were playing Japs and Commandos or some similar warlike game – this was some time ago when I was in primary school. Inevitably I was left towards the end, when the real haggling came into play. I suspect some of these children are now career diplomats.

Well, there is nobody else, you will have to take John.

We don't want him.

We don't either.

Well, we will take him because that will even things out as you have more girls.

Yes, life was quite different back in those unreconstructed days. Children probably fight over getting the most culturally and racially diverse team and a 'physically challenged' partner would be a source of pride.

A: You weren't physically challenged were you, John?

JB: When I was still quite young and impressionable my mother took me aside and said:

> *'John, you are weedy. You will have to study very hard and pass all your exams so that you will be able to get a nice indoor job with no lifting.'*

A: Well, ballet schools are a lot more civilised and enlightened and little boys and girls are partnered up according to:

how big a donation their parents give the endowment fund?

love and physical attraction?

spite of the teacher?

their life force aura?

colours of their clothes? – there is nothing worse than a clash

JB: As part of a new controversial development in education I have not faithfully reproduced A's answer here but given the above possibilities. An exciting new interactive part of the book now follows. Choose the above and put them into order of importance. Remember to write in large, firm, indelible writing (you will be saving your second copy of this book for best, remember).

A: Boys are taught partner work from quite a young age. At first they will do strengthening work like push ups and just gentle dancing with their partner like waltzing etc..

JB: Waltzing isn't gentle the way I dance.

A: From here it gradually develops to just holding a girl upright as she balances on her pointe shoes. This then leads to balances on one leg and small simple lifts. Gradually, in a building block type of structure, the boy develops his strength and adjusts to dancing with a girl. It is actually easier for the boy to lift a girl than a sack of something as the girl is also taught how to hold her body, or bend her body to the boy so as to help the lift and make it easier. Coordination between the boy and girl is the most important thing in partner work, not strength (believe it or not). They bend together and as the girl jumps the boy lifts… it's all in the timing.

JB: Being a surgeon, it is perhaps inevitable that I should want to turn to subjects such as Anatomy and Physiology. Some questions probably sound naïve or plain stupid to the expert but are entirely reasonable to the lay person or simple 'man in the street'. The dancer has moved on and may be so wrapped up in the subject that such things are never even thought about. But as we are discussing things like 'questions you might be too shy to ask in public', here is one that comes to mind. Do left-handed ballerinas prefer to spin in the opposite direction to right-handed?

A: A left-handed ballerina will in most cases be a better left turner, but this is never normally a problem. Usually, if a dancer is given a series of steps in class they will be repeated left and right so always working on the weaker side, and in a performance the dancers can normally decide if they would like to perform their turns right or left. Most people opt for right but the Russians, for example, are big left fans. I think it is to do with their training.

JB: Nothing to do with being left wing, then? Perhaps the Eastern bloc just went their own way. I heard that Stalin didn't like the sad ending in Swan Lake so the Soviet version was altered.

A: We explore the stories of ballets in a special section listed on the contents page.

JB: Just what is a coryphée and where have they all gone?

A: There is a glossary where all these terms are explained so that you can delight your friends, confuse your enemies and impress your neighbours.

JB: You must need to be very much in tune with your bodies, keeping them toned to perfection, eating well, and staying healthy. Perhaps that is why ballerinas are usually stunningly beautiful – all that exercise and healthy living. I have often said that the majority of ballet dancers are gorgeous, and perhaps that is the reason.

A: Yes, but you say that about barmaids as well.

JB: True. Perhaps it is the romance of the setting, the music, the anticipation of the performance. Apart from that, ballet dancers and barmaids share little in common. But you must have to be physically very fit and healthy.

A: It is important for dancers to be physically fit for dancing. Too skinny can be a disaster (although some companies don't seem to mind how skinny their dancers get) but then an overweight dancer will be more physically demanding on her male partner. A dancer has to be able to perform a physical job night after night so it is important to eat and sleep well to refuel. Over the years dancing has become a lot more physical and demanding than older times. The lifts are harder and more gravity-defying, men and women are expected to turn more, jump higher, and do fantastical things with their bodies.

JB: How can this be best achieved?

A: Physically speaking, and anatomically, dancers, I don't feel, are given enough information on the upkeep and maintenance of their bodies – considering we make our livelihoods working with them. I was fortunate enough to be given a small anatomy course as I was training but I do know that not very many dancers are given this. I think a basic understanding of bones, joints, muscles, tendons etc. would be very beneficial to all dancers. Most dancers have a loose idea through various injuries they have incurred during their career but I do not think enough emphasis is focused on this area. The main reason for this is that dancing is still very much seen as an art form (which it is, without a doubt) but it is also a physical sport and I feel it needs to be seen a little more like this to understand the demand it takes on the body.

JB: So every dancer really should read our chapter devoted to this?

A: I suggest they cut out the pages from their spare copy of this book and stick some of the information on their fridge, or sleep with it under their pillow!

JB: It is that important! Injuries must be an occupational hazard, even with the best training, though.

A: Injuries are always very common with dancers. Usually they are due to repetition on a weakness or perhaps a little flaw in their technique. Occasionally they can come out of the blue. I fractured my foot during a performance once, which was no picnic! Ballerinas have constant blisters, bruised toe nails, bunion problem etc. from pointe work, but this is something you learn to cope with from a very young age. Ankle, knee and hip injuries are probably most common due to the demands of what we do. Back injuries are also common.

JB: There must be times when you are in pain.

A: Dancers are very good, though, at working with and through pain...we must be sadomasochists! Seriously, just about every dancer I know has pain or injury in some way, you just learn to deal with it. The alternative is to not dance which is never a very attractive prospect if you can help it.

JB: I suppose there is the temptation to take painkillers to relieve the pain and continue dancing rather than remove the cause. Let us now move onto another theme: costume malfunction. This was a term made famous by the Janet Jackson episode where millions of American television viewers were 'shocked and outraged' (their description) when her top fell down during a live transmission from a sports final of some sort. Has a ballerina ever had her dress come off or slipped down? It used to be almost a custom for starlets to 'lose' their bikini tops in the sea at Cannes in front of photographers. Ballet dresses need to withstand quite a lot and seem ever so flimsy, with tiny little straps. Despite being an avid ballet goer for more years than I care to remember I have never seen one ripped off despite the most dramatic lifts and spins. Some must surely be fixed tightly like corsets. These are perhaps trade secrets whose divulgence might compromise the magic and mystery of the art.

A: Problems happen with costumes on a regular basis.

JB: I must have just been unlucky!

A: The stitching has to be very strong and the material usually very stretchy with a lot of give, but even this sometimes cannot withstand the demands which we place on a costume. One time on stage I was in the middle of a pas de deux and I felt all my costume rip down the back. I swear the audience could hear it rip too, it was so loud, but I had no choice but to continue. I tried very hard not to show my back to the audience but it was a tricky pas de deux and at some points it couldn't be helped. That's the beauty of live theatre, I suppose!!

JB: Do you think that might have been the origin of why ballerinas started to bow instead of curtsey?

A: So many questions! I think that this is long enough for the introduction and the reader should dive straight in to find the answer to this and many more items of interest, some of which have probably never even crossed the minds of the less inquisitive.

Message

'A' wears many hats – dancer, education officer, ballet mistress... Something had to give – and it was the job of collaboration. Fortunately others stepped into the breach, otherwise the book, left in the hands of a doctor alone, might have had less to do with ballet and more to do with the audience, parents, fathers and JB's sometimes rather oblique view of life. We hope it remains balanced and READABLE – and not one of those books that is bought and then remains on the bookshelf.

The Stage and Working Conditions

Including:

- **Space, dimensions and surface**
- **Temperature**
- **Refreshment**
- **The glamorous life of a dancer**
- **The 'pecking order' in ballet**
- **Clothes and costumes**
- **Gestures**
- **Music**

Space, dimensions and surface

So you are a wealthy industrialist, banker or somebody who just has money to spare (we realise, of course, that only a proportion of readers fall into this category, but for those of you who don't, then the lottery or premium bonds may always come up). You want to commission a ballet company to put on a performance. Would they fit into your drawing room? Well, there really is no such thing as an average stage, but what is probably more important is the minimum necessary. Again, this can be difficult to gauge because different companies will have different requirements. Do you get the feeling that you are not going to get a straight answer to this? Well, do bear in mind that even professional football pitches are not always the same size!

Interestingly, the space behind what is normally on view i.e. the dancing area, is only a fraction of the total stage area and can extend behind as much as the seating area in front. This is where the various backcloths come down, the sets from the side slide in. This is quite an intoxicating thought when you are sitting in the back row of the stalls – imagine how far away the back of the stage is! Anyway, back to the question. It really depends a lot on the Company and what they can work with. Independent Ballet Wales prided itself on performing at one of the smallest theatres in England – The Georgian Theatre Royal, Richmond, which dates back to 1788. From side to side the stage measures a mere six metres – this can barely accommodate a good leap including take-off and landing. The Company no longer go there, but still visit The Plough Arts Centre, Torrington in North Devon. Until recently this had a stone floor but there is now a wooden dance surface. Thus there are several variables – the style of dance, the company and the attractiveness of the venue itself and likely audience. A room at Buckingham Palace was, after all, converted so that *Les Misérables* could be performed there at the state visit of the President of France. Shall we say that unless you move in these circles and have these facilities, and unless you want a Prima Ballerina flying through the serving hatch into the kitchen or straight through the French windows into that new 'conservatory', then it is probably better to get a conjuror for dear little Courgette's birthday party!

In order to cope with the problems of finding suitable venues, in particular in smaller towns, and in order to bring ballet to those places where it might otherwise not be seen, Ballet Rambert came up with a novel idea. They developed a Dance Unit – a compact mobile group of four dancers, director and technical staff. This 'mini-Rambert' allowed performances in theatres and halls where for space or technical limitations the Company itself could not appear. Where possible, it also allowed the Company to be preceded on tour, giving performances in and around the towns where it was to dance and thus strengthening educational links.

A small point which is not usually considered, but which is quite important, is the sound of the surface – this can influence the choice of what is worn on the dancers' feet. A very hard pointe slipper would make a lot of noise running up and down the stairs which are to be found in Romeo and Juliet, where softer, more worn-in footwear might be more appropriate. This is covered more fully later on in the section on footwear.

The rake of the stage is the term given to the slope from behind forwards. Dancers have to take this into account because the incline can be gentle or steep, depending on the theatre, and clearly can affect their balance. For this reason the rehearsal room in the Paris Opéra has a floor matching exactly the incline of the stage. The Royal Opera House Covent Garden has seven ballet studios – and they are all the same size – 15m by 15m to match the dance area of the main stage. They are kept, as are the surrounding corridors and the like, at the optimum temperature for the dancers – at a 'Goldilocks temperature' – not too hot, not too cold, but just right. In this way, ballerinas may be likened to fine wine. The rehearsal rooms for the opera singers are kept slightly cooler.

With all these variables it would be strange if there was no disagreement. Do not be disappointed – controversy abounds, as exemplified by the events in New York to house both ballet and opera. The refurbishment and redevelopment of London's Royal Opera House is covered in the chapter 'Famous Ballets' section 'Ballet companies and their stages', and you will see how things should be done. In the meantime, just enjoy reading about how the Americans are making a mess of things, and bask in *Schadenfreude*.

The New Yorkers have an arrangement similar to the mother country whereby their opera and ballet are located together – at the Lincoln Center. The story was reported in the *New York Times* 27 Nov 07 and it seems that the New York City Opera gave up on the idea of leaving the Lincoln Center to build its own home after about a year of indecisiveness. The problem is that the Opera and the New York City Ballet share the New York State Theater there, alternating seasons, and they cannot agree on its layout. Chief among the issues was whether to create a centre aisle (the opera was strongly in favour, the ballet adamantly opposed) and how to adjust the acoustics (the opera believes they are in dire need of redress, the ballet is quite content). There have been agreements on creating a larger orchestra pit that can move up and down, upgrading the seating, carpeting and box office and rewiring to improve lighting and media capabilities. The compromise is a modular acoustical system that can be moved in for the opera and out for the ballet, but a spokesman said:

> *The centre aisle is not up for discussion because it had been such an emotional subject.*

It would be wrong to run away with the idea that every company has always been so well provided. When William Ferguson joined Ballet Rambert in 1948 (he spent 33 years with the company preparing scenery and props), wood, canvas and other materials were in short supply, as well as money – there were no Arts Council grants in those days. To make things even worse, there was nowhere to work other than some waste ground in Notting Hill Gate across from the Mercury Theatre.

Temperature

Temperature is important (muscles, warm-up exercises etc). In the early seventies in Leeds a ballet was actually cancelled because the theatre could not be heated to the required temperature. The hardy Yorkshire folk probably did not try throwing much coal on the furnace, considering that the dancers could wear those funny thick socks which seemed so fashionable some time ago called leg warmers. They seem to be based on the tea cosy principle but it might not be that they keep warm legs from cooling, but warm up already cold legs. It is quite variable how long a dancer will take to warm up before a performance – anything up to half an hour seems to be needed.

A more often heard complaint from the public is that the place is too hot. This was especially so before the advent of electricity when theatres were illuminated by gas, but is still a problem, especially when the venues are well attended. When the Royal Opera House was fully refurbished, air conditioning was installed. When you next go, take a look under where you are sitting – each seat now has its own little vent. The eagle-eyed will also notice that the gold leaf is sparklingly bright at the back, but the nearer the stage one gets, the duller the decoration on the walls becomes. This is to prevent unwanted reflection. Note also that the angels on the three different tiers are different. On the upper they represent seven-year-old girls, the middle has fourteen-year-old girls, and on the lower it is quite obvious they are aged twenty-one. In France angels are male, and the French word is un ange (masculine). We will stop now in case when you are next there you become too distracted from the performance! Instead, we can highly recommend Mr Barry Stewart and his team, who offer guided tours of both backstage and front of house

Refreshment

Food is obviously very important. Before acquiring the knowledge required for a work such as this, JB often wondered whether dancers all starved themselves beforehand then went out for a big meal afterwards. It would not seem to be wise to eat a lot and then be thrown upside down, spun around etc. It has not been generally recorded whether anyone has ever thrown up during a pirouette. One could upset a lot of people in a very short time. Nothing to eat for two hours before a performance seems to be about the norm. It is surprising how many dancers smoke, and this may help in denting the appetite and keeping them thin. It is not to be encouraged. An unforeseen consequence of the smoking ban in nightclubs and other dance venues is the appalling smell of body odour which had previously been masked by the smell of cigarette smoke.

The whole question of dancers starving themselves is covered in the section 'Some Medical Asides', but now might be a good time to point out the public perception of a girl who dances ballet to be a delicate, thin, waif–like creature. Opposite the Royal Opera House Covent Garden there is a stature erected by Westminster Council in 1988 entitled *Young Dancer.* The sculptor was Enzo Plazzotta (1921–81) and he has made her look so thin she appears very old and sick. Every neck muscle and tendon can be seen and her limbs are like matches.

To quote Deborah Bull, writing as Creative Director of the Royal Opera House (where she had previously been a successful dancer) in *The Times* 16 December 2010, 'Thin is not a job requirement, it is a trend'. The original *Sugar Plum Fairy,* Antonietta Dell'Era, in 1892, is unlikely to have looked like Kate Moss and presumably she danced the steps perfectly – they were, after all, created for her.

Anastasia Volochkova fell out with the Bolshoi Theatre where it had been claimed in 2003 that she was too tall and heavy – she weighed seven and a half stones (47.6kg)! Undeterred, she allowed the party *United Russia* to use her image in electoral campaigns, more of which can be found in the section on celebrity. Another dancer who lost her job is Mariafrancesca Garritano, who was sacked from Milan's prestigious La Scala for 'damaging the image of the company'. She claimed that her training at its ballet school had led her and many of her fellow students into severe body dysmorphia. She argued that one in five ballerinas now suffers from anorexia and suggested that many were unable to get pregnant as a result.

A dancer's self-image can, it seems, be quite highly (or wrongly) developed. Certainly Rudolf Nureyev, born 1938, seems to have had far more photographs taken of himself as a student in the 1950s Leningrad than one would believe possible. This was before he achieved any fame, but we have pictures of him taken everywhere and in every conceivable pose. Who had the cameras, and how were all these pictures developed? People then had virtually nothing – even thirty years later conditions were such that personal photographs were rare and highly prized. So, good advice is to record everything. If fame doesn't follow, then at least your memoirs will be well illustrated! And of course it is only fair on any future biographer or researcher – at least, that is what JB thinks!

The glamorous life of a dancer

Fame in the arts has long since been a means of social advancement. Probably the best known example are actresses such as Nell Gwyn, who was born into poverty but by dint of her bawdy, bouncy personality (and probably other things as well) attracted the attention of the reigning monarch Charles ll. The Prince of Wales, later to become Edward Vll, was beguiled by the Parisian dancer known as *La Goulue*. For those who did not attract royalty, painters were also available. Hogarth, Gainsborough, Reynolds and Romney all played roles in the careers of actresses that today would be the job of a public relations professional. Once you have hit the top in ballet then there are many more doors which then open, such as meeting royalty (and the rich and famous – football stars and the like). The early Ballet Rambert audiences were very distinguished, as only members of the elite Ballet Club could attend. This included important people from political, artistic and social worlds whom the dancers might meet after the show.

In 1985 The Royal Ballet's Wayne Sleep achieved a first by dancing with a royal princess on stage – there was an 'impromptu' moment at the Royal Gala Performance, Covent Garden when HRH Princess Diana, wife of the Prince of Wales (as she was then) joined him on stage. The Royal Family were apparently not amused and this has never been repeated with any other royals. But who knows, in time ….

Darcey Bussell, now more famous for her role as a judge in television talent shows, mentions how she had an 'all areas pass' from The Rolling Stones. Her portrait, commissioned by the

National Portrait Gallery, hangs in No 10 Downing Street. She was made OBE (Officer of the Order of the British Empire) in 1995, CBE (Commander) in 2006 and DBE (Dame) in 2018. Perhaps a more tangible, (or even a more easily understood!) accolade is when your name is commemorated in a piece of furniture. If so, then Darcey Bussell has hit the top – there is now 'the elegant Darcey walnut dining table'. This is by Steuart Padwick and retails for £3,475 (exc. delivery) and was covered in the *Inner Vision* section of *The Sunday Times* 30 September 2007. The *Daily Mail* had what they named an 'exclusive' – a whole page spread of six photographs entitled 'Darcey Bussell models High Street party wear fit for a diva' on Thursday 8 November 2007, p52 *Femail* Section.

Film appearances can also be numbered in the list of possibilities – Wayne Sleep appeared in *The Virgin Soldiers* – the 1969 film adaptation of Leslie Thomas's novel. Christopher Gable had better luck playing opposite Twiggy in Ken Russell's 1971 film version of Sandy Wilson's *The Boyfriend*. At least he got to dance, rather than mince around as a homosexual National Service soldier. Remember, Wayne Sleep still holds the word record for entrechat douze (more of this later in this chapter – be patient!) so was probably physically more fit that the majority of real soldiers.

Two dancers were immortalised in a small statue to be found in the lobby of the Hippodrome Theatre – home of Birmingham Royal Ballet. It was presented by Francis C Graves OBE DL to commemorate twenty-five years as director of the Birmingham Hippodrome 1978-2003. The statue is a dancing couple from the ballet *Hobson's Choice* – though why he chose this ballet remains unclear!

Another DB, Deborah Bull, has debated at the Oxford Union and gave the Arts Council Annual Lecture for 1996. In 1998 she published two books and was appointed to the Arts Council. The following year she was made a CBE and has received an honorary doctorate from Derby University. She also appeared in a short television series with the writer and comedian Alexei Sayle, demonstrating how dance in all forms can be accessible and enjoyable. This had not been the first exposure of dance to television – far from it! In the 1930s, ballet was identified as perfect for the new medium of television, being a visual art and thus demonstrating what the new technology had to offer. It brought in well-known dancers of the time and by the 1950s was well placed to fulfil a role embodied in the Reithian values of 'inform, educate and entertain'. Relatively few people had actually seen live ballet at that time but 1953 saw Alicia Markova in an extract of *Les Sylphides,* which of course is a ballet without a story, so there was no problem if the viewer did not really understand what was going on. By the 1950s the focus had passed on to Margot Fontaine, although she had actually appeared on television at the age of eighteen in the 1930s for the fledgling service, and was Dame Ninette de Valois' greatest discovery at the Vic-Wells ballet school. During the 1950s she was bringing the high art of ballet to the public and being treated like royalty. *The Nutcracker* became a popular Christmas offering (surprise, surprise) and in 1958 was adapted in full for British television. In the following year *The Sleeping Beauty* was broadcast live. By the 1960s The Royal Ballet had signed up for new TV collaborations, further extending the exposure of ballet.

After Dame Margot Fonteyn had left The Royal Ballet she kept herself busy as President of the Royal Academy of Dancing and Chancellor of the University of Durham.

Lynn Jezzard rose through the ranks of Northern Ballet Theatre to become principle in many of their classic productions. Following this classical career she went on to dance with Wayne Sleep with his company in various pantomimes and then in the *Phantom of the Opera,* finally becoming its resident choreographer.

In contrast, the eagle-eyed will notice that sometimes in a programme the full list of dancers in a company is missing – but never the list of benefactors! Tracy Brown, of The Royal Ballet, has had her name spelled Tracey – but her career didn't seem to suffer, thank goodness. Names do seem to have a certain importance – it is interesting to note that the great Dame Ninette de Valois OM CH DBE was born in Ireland 1898 as Edris Stannus. She was referred to in deferential terms until her death in 2001 as 'Madame'.

For its post-war visit to the USA, Sadler's Wells Ballet was supported by leading British fashion houses with specially designed dresses and coats for the dancers to wear outside the theatre. They chose who was to wear which label by drawing names from a hat.

But all is not beer and skittles. In 1993 during a French tour a gala was given in the presence of HRH Princess Margaret, followed by a reception at the Hôtel de Ville in Paris. Only a few of the invited guests were allowed to sit down at the meal – the dancers who had given performances in three ballets that evening had to make do with canapés in an ante room. This was at least an improvement on the 1939 tour when at a reception 'given in their honour' at the British Embassy, none had been invited to dine.

Perhaps that was a reflection of the long-held belief of the stage 'not being quite respectable'. Noel Coward was not alone in advising 'don't put your daughter on the stage'. Whenever the Victorian painter George Frederick Watts was asked about his brief marriage at the age of 46 to the 17-year-old Ellen Terry, he explained that he had acted from the highest motive – to protect an innocent young girl from embarking on a theatrical career.

There was a lot of controversy at the ROH about how performers, both ballet and opera, were paid far less than stage hands. Perhaps there is the feeling that as they enjoy it so much, and there is no shortage of applicants, they can manage with less pay. The same sort of thing seems to have happened for generations of young nurses. Fame may be perhaps thought of as a substitute for money – but of course it does not pay the bills. During the late thirties ballet dancers were invited to produce some performances for the fledgling television service – though the number of television sets in the country was in the low thousands and the transmission was limited to Greater London. So the audience was probably in the hundreds. The fee was thirty shillings (or, as we used to write, 30/-) which is £1.50 for two performances. Not a lot, you might think. But that was the wages for a week for a labourer. The same dancers a few years previously (1932) were receiving a salary of ten shillings per week – this is actually 50p – but it was the same as the old age pension at the time. But looking at it from a different point of view, during the early 1930s of Ballet Rambert pay per performance was three shillings and sixpence for boys and two shillings and sixpence for girls – the dancers could hardly pay for their bus fares.

In an interview with a member of the Corps de Ballet, Iohna Loots, on a Christmas Day television programme on The Royal Ballet, speaks of her anxiety about not being able to afford a mortgage at the age of thirty, and other financial worries.
But let us not dwell exclusively on financial rewards.

Sir Frederick Ashton received not only a knighthood, but was also a holder of the Companion of Honour, one of the highest honours bestowed by HM the Queen. Following his death, a memorial service was held for him in Westminster Abbey.

It must not be thought that accolades and prizes are always given out in a fair and just manner. That is not to say that your authors begrudge anybody receiving these – just that it is hardly a foolproof scientific method. Rather than carp on and lay ourselves open to charges of jealousy etc., let us just simply state the following taken from the world of literature. Why literature? Well, one of the world's most prestigious awards is the Nobel Prize. And one of them is awarded for literature. The reason the Swedes have the honour of bestowing one of the world's most prestigious awards lies in the history of explosives, warfare etc. Anyway, think of the great writers the world has produced. There have been six writers who have won the Nobel Prize for literature who have been Swedish. None of them on your list? Exactly.

Perhaps now would be an opportune time to look at the rank structure of the dancers within a ballet company.

The 'pecking order' in ballet

'Ballerina' seems to be the most common term for the layman to apply to a woman who dances ballet, but in Tsarist Russia this was an official ranking. In fact, the appellation 'ballerina' is strictly for a principal female dancer who has 'proved' herself in the leading classical roles of a company's repertory. Where there are a number of ballerinas, the leading one is called the prima ballerina. By rights, only the most exalted of the great ballerinas may use the title 'prima ballerina assoluta'. This was an official ranking which was only bestowed on two dancers in Imperial Russia (Pierina Legnani and Mathilde Kschessinskaya, for those readers bursting to know!). There is a memorial tablet in St Paul's Church, Covent Garden describing Tamara Karsavina as an 'assoluta', but this is INCORRECT. The accolade was, however, officially given to Maya Plisetskaya and Margot Fonteyn. Phew, that was tricky, wasn't it? Especially the names. The reader is advised not to memorise them, unless it is intended that they are to be used in some strange form of balletic pub quiz or for the purpose of winning money from impressionable young balletomanes who have not had the benefit of reading this book. But this action cannot be condoned.

Moving from the top back down to the beginning, we have the Corps de Ballet. In essence, the Corps de Ballet refers to all dancers below the rank of soloist – it may perhaps be likened to the chorus of an opera. The French, however, are different (surprise, surprise!). At the Paris Opéra, it means the whole company. That is from the newest of les quadrilles (the lowest rank which they have) up to the étoiles (star dancers).

The Corps is the bedrock of a classical ballet company and reflects its style and schooling. Members dance together the same steps in unison, providing the background and support for the central characters. It is hard work, and many dancers do not progress beyond this level. This gives it an unfair 'poor relation' feel, but their role is important and their performance can make or break a show. It must be remembered that, unlike more solitary arts such as painting or writing, dancers work together. They are always conscious of each other and often subordinate their individual talents and efforts for the unity of the whole. The Corps provide an important image of symmetry – our eyes are drawn to this as they balance the stage performing in unison, sometimes split into two groups dancing the mirror image of each other.

But don't think it is as simple as that – next we have the Coryphée (this comes from 'coryphaeus' – leader of the chorus) who is a leading member of the corps. The designation is only used in Britain, France and Russia and seems to be dropping out. Although we might not see the term so often in our programmes, it is still adopted by managements when grading salaries for dancers. Thus the Corps is divided into grades – first year, second year and so on with the fifth year dancer being a coryphée and immediately below the rank of soloist.

Looking back over theatre programmes to the 1970s, it is apparent that not only is there variation between companies, but that things change over time. Back in those days we find

artist   coryphée   solo artist (or soloist)   principal

London Festival Ballet managed to insert another level above soloist – that of senior artist.

By 2000, coryphée has disappeared – Birmingham Royal Ballet has:

artist   first artist   soloist   principal

By 2007, the same company had added another rank, that of first soloist

artist   first artist   soloist   first soloist   principal

One would have loved to be a fly on the wall when this was announced and learn the response of those who thought they were going to be promoted from soloist up to principal and then find that they had another rung – first soloist – to endure. Or perhaps it was just another way of holding down salaries by granting another title. The reason is shrouded in mystery! It has to be said, though, that The Royal Ballet has the same: after soloist comes first soloist.

In a very democratic, though not as informative manner, some transatlantic companies simply list all their dancers, a trend which seems to be taking on here. Sometimes this is in alphabetical order, as with Ballet Rambert and The Scottish Ballet. If it is not in alphabetical order, then one wonders what subtle rules unknown to the general public are employed. Although there is space on the page, The Royal Ballet lists only its principals, first soloists and soloists – anybody further down the line than that is anonymous. They do manage to put in Principal Character Artists, though.

The training needed before beginning a professional career in classical ballet will take seven or eight years, taking the child to the age of seventeen or eighteen. Assuming success and acceptance into the company (which is by no means assured), the student will be able to participate from the start in the full works of the Corps de Ballet. Here she/he will spend two or three years of apprenticeship before being tried out in minor soloist roles. It is a fact of life, as previously mentioned, that most dancers do not progress beyond the Corps in this rather pyramidal career structure. For the lucky 'chosen' ones, it will be some time after taking solo parts before being given the responsibility of a principal role. There are, of course, exceptions where the promotion is much faster. Ill-educated people may say 'meteoric' – but meteors plunge ever downward towards the earth, so the reader is cautioned against this metaphor.

Male dancers have been traditionally divided into three types according to their physique:

Danseur noble – a noble bearing with elegant proportions and long legs; dances principal roles.

Demi-character – a little more compact in physique; his dances are quicker to show off his brilliant footwork, bounding jumps and fast turns.

Character – originally called comique (or even grotesque), these dancers are of stocky build and were perfect for playing beasts or fantastic creatures when ballets were mostly about mythological subjects. Their forte now is more likely to be character or comic parts.

Wayne Sleep, who became a principal dancer with The Royal Ballet, was at 5′2″ (1.6m) the shortest male dancer ever admitted. Apparently, he left the initial auditions early and so missed out on the physical exam. If he had stayed he would not have been accepted! Owing to his lack of height, directors struggled to cast him and many choreographers created special character roles especially for him. The role of character dancer is often taken on by an older male dancer who can no longer perform the more energetic roles danced in his youth. This seems to be an opportunity less readily available to female dancers, or to the tall. Whilst considering the drawbacks of short stature, we must consider the opposite end of the spectrum. What happens when a dancer is too tall? As in all things, the situation has changed and nowadays there are dancers who are quite tall. It has not always been like this. Aficionados of Morecambe and Wise may remember their film *That Riviera Touch* (1966). If so, then they will certainly remember Suzanne Lloyd, the gorgeous French woman who was working for the criminals and who befriended Ernie after his large win at the casino (some things are timeless!). She was born in 1939 and attended Sadler's Wells Ballet School, but had to leave when she had grown so much she was 1.73m tall. She became a show girl and model and was briefly a member of Lionel Blair's dance troupe before her successful film career.

Régisseur – sometimes known as répétiteur – this person usually has overall responsibility for all aspects of the production, including the responsibility of ensuring that the cast know the steps. There is also the responsibility of preserving the repertory in order for performances to take place at a later date. There are two famous examples:

> Nicholas Sergeyev had been a régisseur of the ballet at the Mariinsky Theatre in Leningrad from 1904 to 1917. On leaving Russia following the 1917 Revolution, he brought with him his notation books, which he used for Sadler's Wells, producing *The Sleeping Beauty* in 1939. Through him the company also received *Giselle, Coppélia, Le Lac des Cygnes* and *Casse Noisette.*
>
> Sergey Grigoriev worked for Diaghilev for the twenty-year existence of the Ballet Russe and then for Colonel de Basil at the Original Ballet Russe. It is thanks to him that much of the early Fokine repertory was preserved.

A penultimate word on glamour made for this book by a dancer is as follows:

> Being in pain when you are a dancer is a problem, but it is not allowed to become one. Most dancers deal with it after the performance – on stage it is all smiles and graceful movements. It can be a little disheartening and there is nothing worse than performing to an audience who have no idea just how much you have put into it.

A final word on glamour – nothing could be more fitting than to conclude by relating something told to JB by a girl employed on the interval drinks counter. She hails from Romania and, as is his wont, JB engaged her in conversation, primarily, but not solely, to obtain material for the book.

Now let us, for a moment, just go off slightly on a tangent. What is the one thing the ponytails tell us about a business, an organisation, an enterprise? Teamwork. Every member has to be valued. We all share in success. You know the sort of thing. This is just to remind you to keep this in the front of your minds.

I asked the little waitress for a story, hoping for some scandal. The only thing which she could relate which she considered shocking was a story she told against herself. There was a matinée performance of *The Nutcracker* one Saturday and a member of the audience had to leave right at the beginning. She left her ticket with a manager, who decided to allocate it to one of the servers, drawing their names out of a hat. Our girl's name was drawn. SHE HAD NEVER SEEN A BALLET BEFORE. To her shame, she fell asleep.

So, next time you are sipping, as I was, a £10.20 glass of Peach Bellini, cast your eye over the serving girls (as I am sure you would be anyway!). Many have never seen a performance.

In a similar manner, when thinking about other members of 'the team', remember when you are fiddling about prising apart pieces of plastic trying to find the spoon for the tub of expensive Royal Opera House ice cream (£4 at 2022 prices for 130ml/4.58 fluid ounces) that it is only because of her thoughtfulness that she points out it is hidden in a little compartment under the lid. It was during the dreadful Covid period that I realised that it really is the little things which count. It is so easy to forget (amongst all the mortality statistics, etc.) the small gestures of kindness which make us human and life worth living. I had a period where instead of working from home I had to be elsewhere and this involved staying overnight in a hotel. House-keeping had folded the loose end of the toilet roll into a triangle tucked into the top. A selfless act of generosity, the effects of which she will not personally see, but which I hope she knows are appreciated. It is a service I had been denied during the long months of being at home.

Clothes and costumes

Queen Victoria was well known for her command of French (as is our current sovereign) and used to liberally lard her writing with it. French was of course the language of diplomacy, the culinary arts, the casino, as well as ballet. It is for this reason that this book will keep to traditional terms, which are in fact used worldwide in ballet. English is, of course, an international language and the lingua franca of commerce, aviation and warfare. French has, we are sure you will agree, a certain 'je ne sais quoi'. The Americans, once again, seem to slightly miss the point. They refer in their restaurants to the main course being the 'entrée'. Nowhere does this occur in Francophone lands – in the restaurant of the Musée d'Orsay there are two menus – the English had 'starter' where the French had 'entrée'. One wonders what the Americans actually think 'entrée' actually means. The Greeks seem to be getting their own back – couscous – so good they named it twice. Similarly, any dessert ordered in the USA 'à la mode' – comes with ice cream. They think this is what it means – we have yet to meet one who considers 'mariage à la mode' to be something to do with Häagen-Dazs. This is a digression, but before returning, just one final snippet on the peculiarities of language. In French, roulette (the game) is the same word as roulette, the suitcase on wheels. An appropriately vaguely worded receipt *may* fool the taxman, but it is doubtful.

It would be folly to miss out in a section like this a valuable piece of advice based on practice in costume departments. The best way to fold trousers on a coat hanger is not the way most people usually do it. The conventional way is to hold the trousers up at the waist and then slide the two legs through the hanger so that the cross piece lies across the middle – about where the knee would be. The astute-minded amongst the readers and those with a keen sense of spatial awareness will realise that the outer part of the leg material is lying against the wood. If left for a year or two (as can happen in some costume collections) then a mark will be left. The better way is to hold the trousers up not by the belt but by the opposite end and then fold one leg around the crosspiece and then the other on top of this. Thus the inside of the trouser is against the wood, not the outside.

Interactive section

In yet another innovation, the editors have allowed the book to send a message to readers who may write in with any answers they may find to the following quandary. JB has always appreciated the beauty of women but has noticed that over the past few decades their appearance has not changed dramatically other than the vagaries of fashion. In particular, regarding hair. Yet, in the past, shops, magazines and catalogues were full of hair curlers. Nowadays hair straighteners are everywhere. But hair seems the same – either straight or curly depending on the woman's choice.

What to wear on the feet?

At first this may sound like a rather strange question and the authors are aware that the impatient reader might already be skimming ahead, thinking that the obvious answer is a shoe, one for each foot. Well, those still confused by the mistranslation which had the English-speaking world labouring under the misconception that Cinderella danced in a glass slipper, it might be wise to take this carefully and slowly. You see, there was probably no difficulty in reading the previous sentence where we mentioned a slipper, was there? No jarring, no grating of teeth, like when we hear Americans referring to McDonalds as a restaurant. Ballet footwear should more accurately be called slippers as they are derived from the light silk slippers worn by the fashionable to dances in the nineteenth century. The French still call them 'chaussons' (slippers) rather than 'chaussures' (shoes). JB always calls them slippers. While we are on the subject of French, your important phrase in this language is 'mon pote paiera'.

The second important fact, and ballet authorities are divided as to whether this is more important than their name, is that THEY HAVE NO RIGHT OR LEFT FEET. That is correct – when they are new they are interchangeable until the dancer works them in and decides which to use for which foot. Hopefully one for the right, and the other for the left.

There are two main sorts – soft and blocked (pointe) slippers. The soft are worn by boys and men and are made from very light leather lined with canvas. The undersole is much smaller than the sole of the foot. The consequence is that the toes and part of the heel stand on the upper leather which is turned under. Actually, they are first constructed inside out, with the maker using metal pincers to creates pleating at the toe. It is then stitched to join the sole to the upper by means of a wax thread.

The soles should be thin and flexible so that the dancer can arch his instep and stretch his toes unimpeded. Girls wear the same sort of soft slipper when they are beginning – if their footwear is too rigid, then the foot muscles cannot exercise properly and do not develop strength.

Pointe slippers (Fr. 'sur la pointe' – on the point) are similar except that they have reinforcement between the outer and inner soles to give support to the lower arch of the foot when standing en pointe. Contrary to some people's belief, they do not contain a large piece of wood at the toe. In fact the maker forms the block by hand, building it up layer upon layer using hessian triangles, paper and glue. The toe is also reinforced with an extra layer of canvas hardened with paste and is squared off to form a little flat area to balance on. Ideally the slipper should be weak and the foot strong – but dancers want a lot of wear from their footwear. Thus the toes tend to be over-blocked and the soles almost rigid. They have to be broken in – sometimes by being hit with a hammer!

Once stitched, the pointe slipper can be removed from the last and 'turned' right side out. The insole is then inserted and the shoe put back onto the last. At this stage of the making process the glue in the block is not yet dry and hard and so can be shaped by the maker with a smooth hammer. Finally, it is 'baked' overnight in an oven. Once hardened by this, the dancer's individual requirements can be attended to. Vamp, side and back are measured and marked by hand prior to the cutting down and binding of the shoe.

In order that they stay on the foot (they have no shoelaces, after all), there is a little draw string. This is tied at the centre front and the edges tucked in. This is usually enough for the soft ones to stay on whilst dancing. If not, then a narrow piece of elastic can be stitched across the upper instep. This is fine for the soft slippers, but for pointe there is a metre of ribbon which is crossed first in front of the ankle, behind, then once more in front and finally tied just on the inside of the ankle with the ends tucked away. A final surprise for the fathers and brothers who know nothing about this at all – they are sold without ribbons or elastic, which are considered a matter of personal preference. These have to be bought separately and sewn on by the dancer herself – and even in the most famous companies, there is no ballet equivalent of football's boot boy who cleans and mends! This knowledge (or in modern idiom this 'intelligence') somewhat spoils the effect during the television programme where a member of the Corps de Ballet, The Royal Ballet was being interviewed about her pay, work conditions, promotion prospects, etc. She was sitting sewing. A tear came to JB's eye as he almost reached for his cheque book. Almost – he is a Yorkshireman. Anyway, the sentiment was misplaced – they ALL sew their footwear.

Similarly there is nobody but the dancer herself to polish them up. In fact, they don't actually need polishing so nobody is needed for that. They do need something to stop slipping, and that is where rosin comes in. This is the solid residue from crude turpentine after the oil has been extracted and is used on the soles of the dancing slipper to prevent slipping. This is usually by means of rubbing them in a box of rosin in the wings of the stage. It can also be applied directly to the stage where necessary.

We now have a personal observation from a mother (who clearly hasn't taught her daughter to get on with things on her own – we thought children liked to be independent!).

> *Sewing in of elastic into slippers is no easy task. I have attempted this on several occasions with varying success. The difficulty lies in getting the tension correct – too loose and the slipper flies across the stage, too tight and the foot bulges beneath and below. Ribbons are easier – it is a bit like tying a joint of beef with string.*

This is an analogy which might be lost on some of the readership. JB has tied neither ballet ribbons nor joints of beef and, until learning of this, had thought himself quite a worldly chap. A member of the Corps can get through ten pairs of ballet slippers per month. Remember, the performances we see are but a small proportion of a dancer's work life. In The Royal Ballet every member spends two hours per day in warm up, exercise, etc. A soloist can get through 10–15 pairs and for a principal 'there is no limit!'

The firm *Freed of London* (which has furnished much of the information here) makes some 250,000 pairs of pointe slippers (they themselves call them shoes) in the traditional 'Turn Shoe' method each year. Each is painstakingly handcrafted by a highly skilled maker. Two thirds of them are made to a dancer's individual specifications – specifications which require accuracy to within 3 mm.

We reproduce some of their advice for fitting:

> *The starting point is your current walking shoe size. Freed's lasts are fairly close to street sizes in length and it is usual to wear the same size or slightly smaller. It is most unusual for a dancer to wear Freed pointe shoes larger than her walking shoe size. However, if it is intended to wear toe sponges or similar this can alter the length by a half size.*
>
> *Freed Pointe Shoes are available from stock in four widths, so it should therefore never be necessary to wear the wrong length to get the correct width. To check the width you should look at the bare foot flat on the floor and pointed forward. The fitting across the metatarsal can then be gauged. Both shoes must always be tried*

on. Initially, one should look at the 'fit on the flat'. When you are standing with weight on the feet and knees bent, your foot will be at its largest proportion. The shoes should feel snug but not pinch, and the dancer should feel the block 'cupping' the toes. You should be able to feel all three points of the foot's triangle on the floor, i.e. under the little toe joint, the big toe joint and the centre of the heel. At this stage the side seam is also checked for tension.

The foot should then be placed en pointe without transferring body weight. The suitability of the shoe's width can be seen by checking whether the outer sole of the shoe remains flat against the pad of the dancer's heels. If the sole twists away from the foot, then this indicates that the shoe is too narrow. Check also that the block contains the toe joints.

The dancer then goes en pointe, transferring the body weight forward onto the toes. Help and encouragement should be given, particularly to a beginner. The dancer must not either relève or rise through the foot. Instead, taking both hands, one should assist her to 'climb' one foot, then the other foot, onto pointe. In this position, the toes are draw back slightly to give the feet additional support and the foot will naturally curve. The consequence is that the foot is shorter in length than when the dancer is standing flat. Therefore when en pointe the shoe will have a slight excess of satin in the heel area. This will be taken up when the dancer comes down. If the outer sole of the shoe extends beyond the pad of the person's heel, the shoe is too long.

It was pointed out bitterly by one mother that a custom made ballet slipper was actually less expensive than a pair of required formal school shoes for her daughter! Perhaps the case is that ordinary children's shoes (despite being zero-rated for VAT) are just far too expensive compared to times gone by. Dame Alicia Markova recalls that she was told by Marie Rambert that everyone was to get six shillings and sixpence (32.5p) a performance but she was to receive 10/6 (as we used to write it in those days!). This was because she needed a new pair of shoes for each Sunday night show and those alone cost 6/6. There is no doubt that a pair of standard school shoes for girls from an 'ordinary' manufacturer are expensive, but more exotic ones – the so-called 'designer shoes' –can cost more than double. One wonders who 'designs' non-designer articles. Perhaps they just evolve spontaneously. It could be that they come into being as a result of some committee, the names of the members of which have to be kept secret. Or perhaps they really are designed, but the designer is so shy that anonymity has to be maintained. Who knows? Who cares? Certainly not JB.

Another piece of information of dubious relevance was the snippet from a 1950s programme shown recently by the BBC (*Ballrooms and Ballerinas: Dance at the BBC* Feb 2022). This was a demonstration between the relative weights of dancing shoes. That of the Russian ballerina Ulanova was measured and found to be heavier than its British counterpart. No explanation was given as to why this was the case.

Dancers put on their costumes about thirty minutes before a performance – and it can be a complicated job. As the clothing has to be able to be worn by a range of dancers, who obviously come in different sizes, one may find up to four sets of hooks and eyes for fastening. There are thirteen sections of lace on a tutu, an item first worn in 1832 by the ballerina Marie Taglioni. Every so often there is a reaction against it, though the often predicted 'revolution' against it rarely seems to come to pass. The most recent appears in an autobiography, *Built for Ballet,* where Leanne Benjamin, the Australian-born former ballerina, revealed she did not like wearing the garment. This was reported in the *Daily Mail* (9 Jan 2022) along with several photographs of her, some wearing the offending garment, which she 'fell out of love with during her career'. The artistic director of the Australian Ballet, David Hallberg, considers that his dancers are now equally happy to step away from the tulle skirts to try something new. For many productions, of course, this is not difficult as they are set in modern times with costumes appropriate to the era. Jo Meredith, the creative director of the UK's National Youth Ballet, also prefers gender neutral outfits to tutus for her production of Kurt Weill's *The Seven Deadly Sins*, holding the view that forgoing the tutu works for her production, because the ballet is set in the 1930s and the cast would be in tuxedos. That is not to say that the rather extravagant newspaper headline should be believed:

> *The tutu, a staple for prima ballerinas, may well be about to pirouette into the history books, as several dancers and artistic directors have said they're keen to move away from the traditional skirt.*

Some have judged it to be too restrictive, both for the body and for the art form – this view surfaces every so often but rarely seems to gain much traction. However, other forces may be more persuasive. Leanne Benjamin, who is now retired, says that although she does not pretend to speak for everyone, but added because tutus were a style of costume, they could be swayed by society's conversation on gender, and that traditional ballet heroines could get new, modern attire to fit changes in society. We shall no doubt see and time will tell. In case anybody is considering reducing the amount of clothing worn, they will not be outdone by the so-called enfant-terrible of his generation, the award-winning Canadian choreographer David St-Pierre. His work 'Un peu de tendresse, bordel de merde' (A little tenderness, for crying out loud) is about the search for love and the human form, and features 20 dances entirely naked. JB saw it in 2011 and it left him with the conviction that he really must lose weight and take more exercise!

Although many of the classical ballets are over a century old, the style of costume has, as with fashion, altered. A famous example of how the pace was forced is when Rudolf Nureyev decided he didn't like the baggy trousers his role demanded. He wanted to wear tights, which he considered showed his physique to better advantage. This was right at the beginning of his career with the Kirov in Leningrad. He came to this decision during the interval. The dancers postponed their return to the stage and the interval was extended – and extended. Finally the management gave way and he was allowed to appear in tights. This wasn't really appropriate to the character – but since then male dancers have tended to wear tights, no matter which role they are dancing.

Clothing is a form of wrapping that serves to display both the signs differentiating us from others and those which indicate our membership of the group. The female body has always been subjected to reshaping to fit the aesthetic appeal of each period: corsets and girdles compressed whilst panniers, hoop skirts and bustles were used to produce the opposite effect. The French have a saying that one must suffer for beauty. This was certainly the case in Victorian times when corsets achieved such a level of tightness that they pressed upon the liver and gallbladder, causing serious medical effects.

To quote Cristóbal Balenciaga (1895-1972), the Spanish fashion designer who was established in Paris in 1937 until his retirement 30 years later:

> 'A fashion designer must be an architect for perspectives, a sculptor for shapes, a painter for colours, a musician for harmony, and a philosopher for a sense of proportion.'

Or, as JB always says: 'When you are good-looking it does not really matter what you wear.'

Regional dress

Towards the end of the 19th century the wearing of regional costume by country people began to decline and examples began to be collected in museums for posterity. However, regional dress was not consistent and tended to change with time. Some which are accepted as typical of a region, and may be still worn on festive occasions, may in fact have been recreated from unreliable 19th century models. Nowhere is this more apparent than Scottish tartans, many of which were created in the 19th century following a fashion started and supported by Queen Victoria.

Trades apparel

Work clothes have always been associated with function, with working garb being made from hard-wearing fabrics. Uniforms facilitated recognition, not just for the military. Clothing worn by nursemaids survives not only because the wearers were turned into walking adverts for their profession but also to show to others that their employers had engaged them.

Youth culture

It is interesting to note that wearing trousers without a belt and shoes without laces derives from standard prison rules in the USA. It originated as a sign of solidarity by disaffected black youths with their prison brothers – something not usually known by current followers of the fashion. There are several places in the USA where trousers at half-mast are forbidden – which of course only adds further impetus. It was only when newsreaders, the headmaster, etc. took to wearing sideburns that the young stopped. So get to it, Jeremy Paxman, Andrew Marr etc. – have your nose pierced!

Gestures

Much of interpretive dance requires the use of gestures which, to the initiated, can convey great subtleties of meaning. This is, of course, nothing unique to ballet – or indeed to the Arts. In our everyday lives the raised eyebrow (perfected in the Surgical Operating Theatre where the rest of the face is hidden by cap and mask), the movement of the mouth, fluttering of the eyelids are all well-known and learnt from an early age. The Covid restrictions which made us all into mask-wearers may well have developed and refined this technique. Time will tell.

There are props with which to develop these movements. The best known is probably the fan, which had its own stylised ritual. We say had, because we think of this object as something from the past, but there are fan shops to this day in Spain. To experience this beautiful object to its best, the ballet *The Sanguine Fan* cannot be bettered. Umbrellas and parasols often achieve similar effects, and the Museo del Traje in Madrid has a good collection of both, including a marquesa. This, which had both modern and oriental influences, came into fashion in the mid-nineteenth century and was small with an articulated shaft – so was particularly expressive. It remained in fashion until about 1920 – and is surely due for a comeback. If only a fraction of the readership of this book asked for one for Christmas…….

Props such as fans or umbrellas are certainly not essential, and are not commonly used in ballet. The arms, legs, inclination of the head, etc. when skilfully used can convey not only emotion but a story. Gestures which cumulatively produce the communication form of mime have, like most other forms of communication, rules. Mime has its origins in the work of the Italian Commedia dell'arte. It became strictly codified in the nineteenth century repertory where a set sequence of gestures was required to explain certain narrative points – the audience was expected to understand this language.

This is in contrast to the present day where mime is regarded as a kind of wordless acting to convey meaning to the audience through gesture and facial expression during the dancing. A natural dramatic expressiveness has been advocated by all the great reformers in ballet's history, in the twentieth century a great advocate being the Russian Michel Fokine (1880-1942). The idea is that dancing should convey meaning and not just be a series of technical feats.

It was not always so – in the nineteenth century choreographers would hold up the dance sequence so that the story could be told in an isolated mime sequence which was intelligible to the audience of the time but is probably incomprehensible now.

As far back as the eighteenth century, mime was preserved in various forms of notation (the notation of dance movements is covered in a special section). There was, for example, a stick figure system developed by Carlo Blasis, the founder of the Italian school of mime in Milan. Just like the systems used for choreography, these were often only understood by their developers, and eventually became lost. The Royal Ballet was fortunate as, just after the Second World War, they had the services of the great Russian ballerina Tamara Karsavina. Now, where has that name come up? We know what you are thinking. She appears just a few pages before in the section devoted to pecking order. She reproduced many of the mime sequences for Ninette de Valois' productions of the Russian classics. Nowadays there is a concise way of mimetic gestures together with the choreography using Benesh Movement Notation.

The order of expression follows that of the French language:

> 'I love you' becomes 'je vous aime' (I you love)
> i.e. the order is changed.

Mime is then, essentially, a codified system of gestures but with the difference that, as ballet is danced to music, so the gestures are also choreographed. In the current style of ballet the dancer does not pause or halt whilst a mime action is being performed. They are also to the audience as a whole rather than a specific individual, as would be found in signing language for the deaf. Thus they need to be emphatic, deliberate and slower. The same applies, but even more so, in helicopter handling. Except, of course, that there are no gestures for kissing, marriage etc – or at least not known to JB, who has had a great deal of military experience.

Most ballet mime consists of imitative gestures and it does not need a genius to realise the mime actions for a baby, love, marriage. In fact, many of the gestures used in ballet are often used in everyday life, sometimes subconsciously. The reader may be surprised to read this – but notice what happens when somebody is speaking on the telephone and has to gesture to somebody else – or in a discotheque – or anywhere where background noise or distraction requires an alternative to speech. But bear in mind that in Bulgaria they shake their head for yes and nod for no!

Mime gestures are much easier to demonstrate than to describe, but the intelligence and reading powers of our readership is higher than that of lesser books, so a few descriptions will not go amiss.

- Marry: point to fourth finger of left hand with index finger of right (of course, in some countries on the continent the wedding ring is worn on the right hand, which once led one of your authors into a little difficulty)
- Listen: hand to ear
- See: hands to the eyes
- Love: hands clasped to the heart (universally recognised to be on the left!)
- Ask: hands clasped in a pleading gesture
- Swear: (as in affirmation rather than profanity!) left hand on heart, right arm raised with the palm facing the audience, fingers and thumb clenched but first two fingers pointing upwards.
- Dance: circling the arms above the head
- Death: place one hand, then the other on the opposite shoulder, then fling both downwards dramatically crossed in front of the body
- Mother: cradle both arms across the body

Gestures not described above and discovered by the reader:

....

....

....

....

In an as yet untried experimental venture, the reader is encouraged to tear out these pages (from their second copy – keep the first copy for best) and take it with them whenever they go to a ballet. Whenever a gesture is seen, then place a tick by the appropriate entry. Add new entries for gestures not described above! When the page is full award yourself a prize of five pounds!

Music

You, dear reader, may be wondering why in such a book devoted to ballet (or dance in general) there now appears to be a side track. Well, the reasons are many, and will be related in no particular order of importance. Music is part of life, from casual whistling to the most formal concert. Music is everywhere and it is certainly a Good Thing. It goes without saying that it was a delight to learn more about this art and pass on its subtleties, nuances and sheer joy. Of course, research demanded meeting delightful people in delightful places, and the benefits of this must never be underestimated. Is it important to actually *know* anything about the subject to enjoy it ? Most people get by. Well, of course, if only getting by is your aim, then you could perhaps skip ahead. But remember, even the military know that in a band the trombonists should march at the front. Though whether this was discovered by some tactical theorist or the advice came from neurosurgeons tired of dealing with cracked skulls is lost in the annals of military history. Anyway, a few facts (as in the 'mission statement' of this book – those questions you didn't like to ask) will not go amiss.

For a start, it must be realised that musicians are a little different from us. In an exceedingly well-written discourse a doctor of audiology (*ENT & Audiology News* 2011;20(5):93) argued that they hear pretty much the same as everybody else, but have highly refined listening skills. That is to say the difference between detecting the sound (hearing) as opposed to applying meaning to it. In other words their brain processes sound in a different way from non-musicians.

JB will now relate how his interest was first awakened – like so many things, it came about by chance. I was (once again) in Paris undertaking research, the benefits of which you have possibly already read – the silk shop, hairdressers, Opera (Garnier, Châtelet, Comique and Bastille) etc., in search of an Offenbach operetta, *La Périchole*. It is one of the lesser known ones and I had not managed to find it on DVD, but had thoroughly enjoyed his *La Belle Hélène* at the Essaïon Theatre where the 'orchestra' consisted of a single pianist – but what a wonderful one. I was reminded of the late lamented Players Theatre – a Victorian music hall revival under London's Charing Cross station where the Master of Ceremonies always used to refer to the 'orchestra', meaning the sole pianist. He also used to announce after the singing of the national anthem (which preceded every performance):

> Gentlemen, you may now smoke,
> Ladies may also smoke, *but only for professional purposes.*

Anyway, yet another digression. In search of a similar experience to *La Belle Hélène* at the Essaïon, I ventured beyond La Périphérique (like going outside the M25 in London) to a small production held in the municipal theatre of the town of Asnières-sur-Seine. A ticket was not hard to come by (it was a Saturday afternoon), nor a place in the very front row. What was surprising, given the venue and the fact that it was an amateur production, was that there was a real, live orchestra. My seat gave me a perfect view of both and, although the operetta was marvellous (I returned the next day for the second and final performance), the activities below the natural line of vision i.e. the orchestra pit, were also fascinating and worth recounting. More importantly for your lonely researcher, cast adrift in a foreign capital, was one of the most beautiful musicians I have ever seen. Readers will have no need to refresh their memory of the description of The Crazy Horse venue in Paris, or of the many other places research for this book has taken JB. Well, if this violinist were to play at The Crazy Horse, the dancers there would complain that her presence distracted the audience away from them! Of course, those readers who have taken my advice and been there will know that they dance to recorded and not live music. It is hard to think how the musicians could concentrate on the score – your humble author, a mediocre pianist under the best of conditions, would certainly have to work blindfolded!

There is a whole opera going on below the stage, with knowing looks, winks and nods exchanged between players, the tension of waiting for the warning light (see later) and the conductor's baton (known, rather confusingly in French as « baguette »). It is a world not readily seen, being blacker that an arts undergraduate's newly replenished wardrobe. The readership should not be denied the same insights into this world as they have had into what goes on above, on the stage itself. Nor will they be! However, it must be said that although your author almost (literally) stumbled on this musician outside the theatre door the second day, words failed him! Experience honed on the battlefield and in the bars and operating theatres of several continents left him tongue-tied and the opportunity was lost. Fortunately we met at another concert and she answered my questions, which I will relate in the form of an interview. You will be pleased (and relieved!) to know that your star-struck author conducted himself quite respectfully, in French, without pestering for an autograph, signed photograph, etc.

JB: I noticed that at times you mouthed various words at key moments – but of course you do not have the libretto, but just the music in front of you.

S: No, and of course mouthing, not speaking or singing, is the key word. I have played for this operetta about twenty times and it is inevitable that one senses key entrances.

JB: Similarly, you know when to get ready to play for the next section ?

S: Yes, but of course one waits for the conductor's baton.

JB: I saw that at this theatre a light came on from the wing to alert him that the stage and cast were ready.

S: Usually there is a smaller light lower down, but the function is the same – a liaison between stage and orchestra pit.

JB: You all wear black, and I suppose this is part of the overall plan of being inconspicuous.

S: The music is above all and you are not meant to be distracted by what we are doing or lights going on.

JB: I can tell from your schedule that life for an orchestral musician can be hectic. Is there any advantage to playing a more unusual instrument?

S: Well, there are more violinists around than there are harpists, for example, but an orchestra needs more violinists. In general it tends to balance out.

JB: And during a performance you are too absorbed to be worrying about the next engagement?

S: Exactly – smokers are distracted from their next cigarette, hunger, thirst, the bathroom are all set aside – a bit like you in the operating theatre.

JB: Thank goodness you don't wear a mask, though.

We have spoken about physical restraints on dancers and inevitably the same question arises in the curious mind as to the position with musicians. The diligent reader will remember how a female friend of JB's had to give up playing the piano accordion. S was asked if physical attributes counted for or against a musician. For instance, was a left-handed violinist at an advantage?

S: No, the right hand is also busy and it is not any easier for a left-hander (the word *gauche* in French means left – in Latin it is *sinister*), which tells us a lot about how these people have been thought in the past. As an aside (yet another one!) the rather old-fashioned English term *louche,* meaning shifty, shady, suspicious, has the meaning in French of *cross-eyed. Loucher* means to squint. The left fingers seem to be doing all the work, but the right (which holds the bow) and the arms all play their bit.

JB: It is a well-known fact, well not as well-known as it should be, that Ear, Nose and Throat surgeons with their delicate fingers and fine touch make excellent lovers. Can the same be said for players of stringed instruments ?

S: Bien sûr (yes, of course). Spread the word!

> *With rings on her fingers and bells on her toes,*
> *She shall have music wherever she goes*
> (part of an English nursery rhyme)

The standard music texts are strangely silent on the role of wearing jewellery by musicians. Certainly JB's medical experience has never included reading a coroner's report of a lady musician being strangled by her necklace caught in the slide of her trombone. Or a tuba player being asphyxiated by aspiration of a tongue stud. In the military, the wearing of (finger) rings is frowned on, the theory being that if caught on the tailboard while the soldier is jumping off the back of a lorry, then the finger will probably be ripped off. S could not come up with any similar cautionary tales in the musical world, but we both came to the conclusion that tympani players were at a definite advantage when wearing self-winding watches.

So you feel up to playing in an orchestra? You practise hard and your music teacher is pleased with your progress. Well, the following might be helpful (and, it is hoped, not too discouraging).

First, the casual observer who has only just recently taken this advice and started to take an interest in the orchestral players might wonder how, with only two eyes (i.e. the normal number humans are allocated), they can keep an eye on the music, their fingers, and the conductor. Well, the answer is simple – you cannot watch where your fingers are! You just have to know.

Second, JB's idea of successfully playing a piano piece – i.e. all the right notes in the right order, is by no means enough. This will be achieved in the first run through of the first rehearsal. And there is no taking it slowly during the difficult parts!

Third, don't even think about it if you do not look good in black!

Ballet and Childhood

Including:

- **What draws children to ballet?**
- **The first ballet I ever saw**
- **Ballet classes**
- **Height and weight requirements**
- **The 'Workshop'**
- **Those left behind**
- **Class**
- **Other forms of dance – including Irish dancing!!**

What draws children to ballet?

For anybody who has to write a 'mission statement' or similar slogan in order to justify their course of action, as seems to be the case nowadays (mercifully, this observation seems a relatively recent development – so the likes of Brunel, Wellington, Stephenson, Nelson, etc. were spared. Otherwise a lot less would have got done!) then the following quote from the famous American dancer Agnes de Mille might be helpful:

> *To dance is to be out of yourself: larger, more beautiful, more powerful. This is power, it is glory on earth and it is yours for the taking.*

JB was taking a small child for a first ballet visit – not surprisingly, as it was over Christmas, the performance was *The Nutcracker.* Within a very short space of time the majesty and opulence of the English National Opera with its so many opportunities to buy things, the glamour of the audience and all the trappings of a visit to the ballet began to weave their magic. The child was entranced. During the interval between mouthfuls of ice cream I enquired as to impressions and whether a career here might be an ambition.

'I would love to work here and dress up and see all the people, but not dance!'

'Why not?'

'They make you stand on one foot, and you could fall over, you know.'

It is interesting how child's speech develops – it its quite right that you stand on one foot – why should adults always say, 'on one leg'? – we 'stand on our own two feet', are 'on our feet all day' – but I digress.

'Well, at ballet school, I think that that is one of the first things they teach you. What would you like to do?'

'I would like to sell the ice creams. You get a nice outfit, and you can see the dancing, people all give you money, and when they switch the lights off then I think you can probably eat the ice cream that is left behind.'

I must say, there was a point to this and it did strike a note. As the afternoon progressed we got on to the subject of clapping. What a strange thing it is, when you actually come to think about it. It is like hitting yourself. In fact, it is hitting yourself. The 'like', as in so many sentences constructed by children, is irrelevant. It is, like, totally redundant, like, man… why don't we just shout 'thank you, thank you' ? – or the equivalent in whatever language we speak, which for children would probably be 'cheers', 'no problem.' The volume could indicate the degree of enthusiasm, just like clapping, but without the pain. Of course at this point we must mention the modern habit of whistling. It is amazing just how loud a sound this can produce right by the ear of the person sitting next to you – and can be dangerous.

While we are talking about applause, why is that people feel the need to stand up? It seems to be becoming ever more common and was only really noticed by JB after he had suffered a broken leg. Once somebody stands up, then nobody behind can see anything. This is especially important for children, but it also applies to the disabled.

In a wholly unscientific way and unrepresentative survey during a surgical conference JB attended, he asked two fellow delegates (it was a very slow meeting) what their early experiences had been. Both former children themselves, I thought their insights might be valuable. How wrong I was – or was I?

The first, Colonel X (not his real name) had only one recollection. It was of looking down at the stage through a pair of opera glasses. I will quote him directly:

> *Getting bored, I turned the glasses the wrong way round so that instead of magnifying, the dancers appeared tiny. I said to my mother – look, they all look like little fairies. Little was I to realise the significance of my statement.*

Clearly Colonel X, perhaps even to this day, feels that ballet consists of effete men in tights dancing around in a rather unmanly way. We will explore this more fully elsewhere as to why on earth people think that for a man to perform incredible acts of physical prowess is somewhat unmanly. Couldn't he see their muscles? – or realise the strength needed to do what they were doing? Yet, he thought that to show an interest, or even to participate in ballet, would make him less masculine and a 'bit of a sissy'. Far better for him to join the rugby scrum, or watch football players kiss and cuddle the moment a goal has been scored. It is truly a strange world we live in, where firmly held beliefs abound whose origin and truth nobody really knows.

The utter wrongness of Colonel X's views was brought home to JB on a military shooting range. Sergeant V is a very solidly built man who used to serve with The Parachute Regiment. In his spare evenings he works as a bouncer in central Manchester. He told me that only once in five years did anybody ever try swinging a punch at him – and he was a rather strange man! You get the picture. We must have had quite a bit of time between shooting serials because we got to talking about this book. I was amazed to learn that his late brother Godfrey Anthony Marsh (died 1998 – they have different surnames) was a professional ballet dancer. 'So what?', you might say. One brother decides his future lies with the British Army, the other with ballet. Well, as with most brothers, there was a certain rivalry – each thought he was tougher, stronger and underwent more fitness training that the other. They grew up in the Moss Side district of Manchester, which refutes somewhat the notion that all potential ballet dancers come from comfortable middle class backgrounds. Anyway, they met up in London and Godfrey matched the pre-parachute training that V was undertaking. Suffice it to say, it involves an enormous amount of running with heavy weights, lifting heavy weights and things which JB could only experience on a theoretical basis. It is one of the toughest things one can do in the British Army. Godfrey managed it all. Then the soldier joined the ballet rehearsals – and in his own words, 'lasted about twenty minutes'. He could not believe how weights (people) could be thrown and caught without any apparent effort. No grunting. It all looked so effortless – because it was based on ability, strength, practice and stamina. Not so effete then, after all.

The second surgeon I asked at the conference, a young lady, couldn't really remember what she had thought as a five-year-old going to ballet classes. She remembers that 'most little girls want at some stage to become ballerinas'. It seems to be a sort of custom or rite of passage that infant girls are sent off to classes. Whether this is to learn ballet, or whether it is a desire to instil a sense of poise, sociability, rhythm, appreciation of music must depend on each family, and the mix will be as varied as the families themselves.

She pointed out that, like most other children, she was taken on a family outing to the ballet – probably *The Nutcracker* at Christmas. So, she enjoyed ballet, went to classes, at some period wanted to be a ballerina, then went on to other things. This is probably the norm – Brownies, a bicycle or pony, school or hobbies intervene.

These two probably reflect the stereotypes held by the public. A man who thinks ballet is a bit effete, a woman who took some classes, enjoyed it as a child, but doesn't go very often because most men in her life won't go because they think it is rather effete...

In a television interview, a member of The Royal Ballet Corps de Ballet gave the opinion:

> Most girls want to dance Juliet in *Romeo and Juliet* – this is a 'girls' special'.

This is perhaps more accurately stated as perhaps a special for girls who are well into the system, have learnt a little how to dance, and have seen a few ballets upon which to make a choice. Perhaps there is too small a middle ground. Of course, if someone has an ambition of becoming an astronaut or a surgeon, then the goal may be achieved, that is the career path taken and the world has another astronaut or surgeon. If not, then one has to reassess one's goals – nobody can be an amateur astronaut, or perform surgical operations in his spare time. But how many people don't become Juliet, but still dance in a ballet setting elsewhere? A tiny proportion reach the top of the slippery career ladder to dance Juliet – and, remember, the dancer in the interview was in the Corps, and had given up hope of any promotion. But she did have a job – she is a dancer in a famous Corps de Ballet. Further research reveals that shortly after the programme was shown (it had been recorded many months before) she was promoted. But what happens to the rest? There is no, or very little, alternative venue. Aerobics and other forms of dance abound – and recent television exposure may increase this trend. Most people can shuffle a little around a dance floor, half remembering the steps to a waltz or quickstep. But ballet is an extreme art form – it is the dance equivalent of neurosurgery, architecture, space travel. It is not so easy to do a bit of it, improvise at home, just 'have a go'.

So we have a rather pyramid-shaped career structure, with fewer and fewer progressing to the higher levels. There is a belief that 'they prepare you to be a star – or they don't'. In other words those who have the potential to reach the very top are selected (perhaps not too overtly) and given roles at an early age (sometimes too early, in the eyes of other dancers!) in which they can develop. The same thing of course happens in the Army – some are selected to go to staff college, then get 'plum' postings in which they can shine, be promoted, etc. It certainly happens in the medical world, especially in surgery where the promising candidates are allowed to assist at more complex operations. They then receive promotion denied to their contemporaries 'who have not done the requisite number of cases…'. It is a competitive world and there are no doubt many other examples. The member of the Corps being interviewed considered that at the age of thirty she had perhaps five more years of dancing left. Perhaps it would be wise at this point, when the reader is beginning to think that dancers must inevitably hang up their slippers and take a second career, that we should mention Dame Antoinette Sibley. She was one of the leading dancers of her generation and at an interview (*The Times*, 17 March 2007) at the age of 68 recounted how she became a mother at 37 and continued dancing for three more years before retiring in 1978. Two years later, after the birth of her second child, she returned to the stage, finally retiring at 50.

Just wanting to attend classes is not enough. There is the problem of expense and accessibility. Ballet classes may be provided as a routine at a private school, but be very difficult to find in some parts of a housing estate where the arts, and especially ballet, are poorly known.

In 1932 Leslie Edwards came to an agreement for classical ballet training – the fee was to be £100 which would be repaid at a rate of 15% of his future earnings until paid off. There was no public funding for students as there is today – though this seems to be diminishing annually.

On the other hand, childhood enthusiasm may be curbed by the parents – JB knows a woman who was denied classes 'because ballet would damage her feet'. She maintains a love of watching ballet and has achieved a reasonably successful career in medicine (well, she ended up as an anaesthetist) and the world of ballet seems to have managed without her. But there are many stumbling blocks in the path of a child wanting to embark on a career in ballet. Perhaps the mother did have a genuine concern for her daughter's feet. But it may well have been an underlying fear that the future chances of success and stability would be much less than if she concentrated her efforts on the more traditional school subjects. Most parents have no objection to a child taking ballet lessons as a part of a general education, but when an absolute resolution develops to take this as a career path, then alarm bells may develop. There is the uncertainly of height. A girl must be prepared to start work seriously before her full height potential is realised.

Iohna Loots joined the school at the age of sixteen with a height of 145 cm and 30 kg (4′ 9″ and 66 lb). To get into the company she needed to be 155 cm (5′ 1″) and she was only 150 cm (4′ 11″). She was advised

If you ever grow, please come back, give me a call

She went home, stopped dancing for six months, then joined a local company. On returning later to London on holiday she called back in and it was noted by Monica Mason, who had given her previous advice to grow, that she had in fact grown and was now 155 cm (5′ 1″). She was offered a position, and considers that her height is now regarded as the benchmark. This does show a certain amount of tenacity and resilience.

Will a child study ballet at the expense of some general education, and then lose interest? It should not be thought, though, that because one specialises in something, then inevitably everything else is set aside. Many scientists are accomplished in the arts, and vice versa. This can sometimes be taken a little far. We all know of the novelist Anthony Burgess (1917-93) through his novel *A Clockwork Orange*. He graduated with a degree in English, but he had aspired to be a composer, librettist and musician, but was very poor at physics. 'So what?', you may think. Well, a qualification in physics was then essential for music students at the University of Manchester. Ballet is not simply about learning certain techniques. A good ballet dancer is more than that, something best expressed in the following:

Iohna Loots, while soloist at The Royal Ballet, held that the ballet is all about the audience in the end, it is why we do it – only for the joy of the audience to make them feel something, sadness, happiness – they are not there to see the technique but for an emotional journey (*The Ballet Association*, 24 September 2008). Nevertheless the acting aspect is only a part. The famous and innovative choreographer Matthew Bourne makes it clear that he does not look specifically for dancers who are interested in acting. He has, however, worked with dancers who have discovered their acting ability and gone on to take straight acting parts as a result. His requirement is for trained dancers due to their ability to be confident in counting. They must hit an expression just for a certain count and then go onto another after counting a certain number of beats. This sort of thing does not throw them but it is unlikely to be found in actors who do not have this training. As he says, 'it is a real skill particular to dancers'.

The first ballet I ever saw

For JB it was a visit to the Manchester Opera House whilst a medical student. I actually thought I was going to see an opera!

It was *Gaîté Parisienne* and the long lost ballet *The Sanguine Fan*. There was a third piece, but it didn't stick in the mind so well and I have to delve through my many boxes of programmes, all lovingly collected over the years. I was a little worried that I might not have bought one, as was sometimes the case (and how one regrets it later!). As a poor student I sometimes thought the proffered list of dancers was an adequate substitute. Programmes cost nearly as much as a paperback novel – and are full of adverts! This is something which is considered in greater depth in a subsequent chapter –'Scandals and Disasters' – but resist the urge to flick ahead! So, the first exposure I had to this art form consisted of wild exciting music and frenetic dance movements, feet movements more complicated than a rapper's handshake, girls of ill repute, drink and debauchery (*Gaîté Parisienne*) and romance, intrigue, double-dealing (*The Sanguine Fan*). It was a microcosm of life itself! I was hooked and visit ballets whenever and wherever I can. There is more about these ballets (and many others) in the chapter *Famous Ballets*.

Ballet classes

Looking back not so far in history we find that dancing was an obligatory social accomplishment and dancing lessons a fact of life in certain strata of society. In fact, the terms 'chassé', 'coupe' and 'pirouette' are not specific ballet terms but steps of the minuet – just as 'envelope' and 'meeting' are not words exclusively reserved for students of Masters of Business Administration. Despite having been on the teaching staff for ballroom dancing whilst on the medical faculty at Southern Illinois University, JB has no knowledge of this dance. Why was ballroom dancing taught as a university course? An interesting question. The answer lies in the requirement for undergraduates to have a pass in sports, and ballroom dancing was included in this category!

It is a widely-held belief among those who actually know something about the subject (rather than parents!), that the choice of teacher is more important than at what age a child begins ballet lessons. Full ballet training is not recommended before nine or ten, but children's classes such as once a week with a responsible teacher can be started from five onwards. There is no truth in the commonly held belief 'the sooner the better', and badly learnt techniques can be difficult to lose. In fact, an untrained pupil who shows promise may well be given preference when it comes to admission to a ballet school over one who has been driven by well-meaning parents to achieve too early accomplishments beyond capabilities. Misleading comparisons may be made with the world of acting where children with appropriate child voices and bodies are needed. But in ballet there are few specific child roles – these are danced by adults. It is important for mothers to understand that it is not in their power to make prodigies, stars or anything else. Before the reader starts wondering why this paragraph reads so authoritatively, and why the authors feel qualified to write in such a manner, we should state that these are the opinions of Dame Margot Fonteyn (born 18 May 1919 and christened Margaret, she attended her first ballet class (in Ealing) just before the age of five).

That is not to say that a start must not be made. In Dame Margot's opinion, both boys and girls are put at a disadvantage for professional ballet if they start too late, but should not (as acrobats) start in extreme youth. Discounting the once-a-week children's classes which serve solely as a preparation, she considered that eight to ten is a good age to start, twelve is still alright and after that every year is more disadvantageous than the last. No pointe work should be attempted until at least two years of study are complete. The information given in the handbook for DanceXchange is that pointe shoes may only be worn in improvers and advanced adult ballet classes and are not allowed in child/teens classes. There is also a 15-minute rule – 'to prevent injury, participants more than 15 minutes late are not allowed into class as the warm-up section will have been missed'.

In St Petersburg the Vaganova Ballet Academy, considered one of the most famous ballet schools in the world, has very strict standards. It is said that no matter how talented, dancers of the wrong height, weight or shape are expelled. It was established in 1738 as the Imperial Ballet School but renamed in 1957 in honour of Agrippina Vaganova, who cultivated the method of classical ballet training which had been taught there from the 1920s. Elements of this have been adopted by many of the world's leading ballet schools. As an aside, the Academy, which produces graduates for the Mariinsky, is located in a beautiful columned building on the 'most beautiful street in the world (Rossi St)', as older guides say. This is a street designed with the golden ratio of its width equalling the height of the building and its length ten times its width.[1]

When Bronislava Nijinska attended the entrance examination there were 214 candidates ready to demonstrate their dance abilities before such greats as Marius Petipa, Cecchetti and Sergei Legat. Twelve girls were accepted. She graduated with seven others, but in addition to her diploma she was enlisted as an Artist of the Imperial Theatre, which assured her of financial security, and of the privileged life of a professional dancer. The competitive world began early!

Pupils enrol at the age of ten, with beginners writing essays on steps they have learnt, describing which muscles are used and how their bodies should move. They are weighed several times a year, with girls who do not keep their weight below 50 Kg (which is considered too heavy for boys to lift) at risk of expulsion. This might seem harsh but as always there are people who considered that the current generation has it easy, with previous times being more difficult. In a *Daily Telegraph* interview published 11 December 2013 the Cuban virtuoso Carlos Acosta, who was 40 at the time, said that young people were always distracted, with technology making their lives easier, in contrast to the discipline of ballet. He felt that the commitment of dancers entering the

1. For this and a host of other things, JB is indebted to Valeria who runs a tour company in St Petersburg – info@vgrtour.ru. Do not worry – it is all translated into English (JB's Russian is not that good!)

profession had diminished. Dance students are not alone in having their weight strictly controlled. It was reported (*Daily Mail* 13 February 2022) that 25 morbidly obese soldiers were sacked from the Army over two years for failing the fitness tests. The latest one, weighing 30 stone (190kg) could not even fit into his body armour. Figures showed that over a period of two years, one in eight personnel were classified as obese, with eight undergoing liposuction procedures.

Height and weight requirements

We have already heard about how Iohna Loots was told that there would be no place for her in The Royal Ballet unless she achieved 5'1" (155 cm). She was told that if ever she should grow, then she should return. She managed to achieve this and considers that the height benchmark is probably herself now. There is a widely-held belief that a girl growing very fast will 'be too tall' and for those reasons gives up ballet. We touched on this in the introduction but, remember, talent will out and there are some very successful tall ballet dancers – Zenaida Yanowsky of The Royal Ballet springs to mind. Darcy Bussell started her career at White Lodge, The Royal Ballet's Lower School, at the relatively late age of 13 (although she had begun ballet classes in her home town at the age of five). Her tallness was considered a disadvantage. She is 1.7m (5ft 7in), making her over 1.8m (6ft) when en pointe. A ballerina can add four or five inches to her height when en pointe. There are those who say her career might well have never got properly started had it not been for the great choreographer Sir Kenneth MacMillan discovering her. She became his muse, and at age 20 the youngest principal dancer in the history of The Royal Ballet.

It is not just the easily measured parameters such as height and weight which can go against someone who ordinarily might be thought competent and suitable. There is that 'extra something', which may not be defined or explained. This was not the case for the otherwise gorgeous Lynn Jezzard (as anyone looking at her biographical photograph in Northern Ballet Theatre's programme would have realised). She was told in no uncertain terms that her ankles had become too large! Despite being one of the Company's premier dancers she thought this was the time to move on. Former airline employees have described how some staff were enrolled into an 'Appearance Management Programme' run by image and grooming officers in order to ensure they were putting on a 'glamorous Emirates face'. The officers would routinely monitor and issue punishments such as pay cuts if they were not meeting the airline's requirements (*Daily Mail* 23 Jan 2022).

While we are talking about physical qualities, we might as well add that, for pole dancing at least, the loss of an arm may not preclude participation. It was reported (*Daily Telegraph* 16 March 2012) that Hong Kong had hosted the International Pole Championship the previous day. Deborah Roach, the Australian winner of the disabled division, is missing an arm 'but always loved to dance'. The reader may well at this point be asking why on earth the subject of pole dancing has been brought up? Well, *The Nutcracker* has always had an Arabian dance set to appropriate music by Tchaikovsky and this usually consists of one male dancer and several females, something which has not gone unnoticed by those who take a particular interest in this sort of so-called exploitation. Mindful of this, a recent production changed the Arabian dance into a pole dance, as this was somehow deemed less offensive (*Daily Mail* 25 Jan 2022)

There are also, of course, exceptions to the age of starting guidelines. Rudolf Nureyev did not enter the Leningrad Ballet School until the age of seventeen and a half, but he realised he was a late starter and had a lot of catching up to do. This is, as stated, an exception. Which proves the rule. This does not mean that once an exception has been found the rule is clearly valid. This comes from a mistranslation of the Latin. The rule is proved i.e. put to the test (like proof firing) when a seeming exception is encountered. Of course you knew that.

Similarly, there are cases of people taking up ballet in middle or late life as an energetic pastime. Retirement can be an opportunity to fulfil dreams thwarted by 'life getting in the way' when one was younger. Remember the adage:

> Retirement – double the spouse, half the income.

The reader is cautioned against the fashion of expecting that anybody can do anything – it is just a question of wanting it enough! This never seemed to be raised in the days when the 'gap year' was called National Service. Now anybody feels able to 'tour Europe and just wait tables'. Perhaps they don't realise that there is a proper three-year training for this. Just watch them in Restaurant Paul (opposite Au Printemps, Blvd Haussmann, just up from La Madeleine – you know the place – it is just opposite where JB gets his ties). You will never feel overworked or put-upon again. This is multi-tasking, efficiency and charm like you have never seen before. Raymond speaks four languages. Jennifer works like she has four arms! JB was questioning a German apprentice who had just started her first year i.e. was right at the beginning of her training at a hotel in Germany. Stuck for something to ask her about, the question was posed as to which glass received the red wine, which the white. She was terribly offended at such a basic question that it might be even possible for somebody not to know that red wine goes in the larger, but could accept that some people might have difficulty realising that rosé wine goes in the white. So we progressed to the Heimlich manoeuvre. One must always, always be mindful when teaching things to contemporaries (in the hope that a friendly exchange of interests and ideas will follow) of the dangers. One is reminded of the psychiatrist who organised a self-help group for his patients who had low esteem. It was so successful that they eventually considered themselves better than him and excluded him.

Recent television programmes (at least within the past few years) have revealed that about two hundred children each year audition for The Royal Ballet School. Twenty-five are selected at the age of about 11, but only about fifteen are still there by the age of 18. The split is about 50:50 girls and boys. At the Central

School of Ballet 25 are accepted – at about the age of 16 for a three-year six day per week course. That year five of them were boys. Deborah Bull, the commentator for one of the programmes (*A Dancer's Body*) revealed that she began her dancing in her home town of Skegness at the Janice Sutton School of Dance in the High Street, which she attended once a week and learnt to hop, skip and dance in circles. At the age of 11 she was admitted to The Royal Ballet School and ten years later joined the Corps de Ballet. She seems to have followed Dame Margot Fonteyn's advice to the letter! In an interview The Royal Ballet soloist Iohna Loots (*The Ballet Association* 24 September 2008) explained that there was no equivalent for her to The Royal Ballet School in South Africa but that she had gone to a high school which offered ballet classes as an optional subject for the last five years of education. Her interviewer, rather provocatively, raised the question of whether we should perhaps get rid of The Royal Ballet junior school (seen as elitist) and put the money into ordinary schools! This was a question that she could hardly answer herself and sensibly did not. Iohna did in fact get into The Royal Ballet School, by getting a scholarship via the Prix de Lausanne.

The 'workshop'

This has been put in inverted commas because it bears no relation to any form of proper workshop, there being no lathes, drills or any form of equipment appertaining to light industry, which of course is the only proper use of the word. Nevertheless, there were emergency repairs to be made beforehand – dancers often have something reminiscent of the bicycle puncture repair kit we used to have as children. The difference is, of course, that rather than having adhesive rubber patches, French chalk and the like, there is needle and thread with which to (re)fasten the ribbons on dancing slippers – or perhaps effect other repairs of a nature too delicate to relate even in a book such as this.

When it comes to learning a technique and then mastering it to perfection, certain generalisations can be made. First, the brain has to see or visualise the motion then, via the nerves, tell the muscles to move appropriately. Practice is needed to make this an easy, fluid motion. A generally held idea was that for most things this equals about 10,000 hours (broken down to 4 hours per day equates to 2,500 days i.e. almost 7 years!). For those who read this with disappointment, be reassured. There is no scientific basis for this commonly held belief. Whilst talking about correcting misconceptions, let us apply this to 'visualisation' and 'seeing'. They are not the same thing. A surgical colleague (Mr J Riddington Young FRCS MPhil) always took great delight emphasising the difference. When performing an operation he was sometimes asked if he could visualise the lesion. He would immediately turn away from the operating table, close his eyes and proclaim:

> *Yes, I am visualising it now, but I will have to dissect a lot further before I have a chance of seeing it.*

It is apparently a great put-down in court.

The first event or pose of the session was the plié (bend) whereby the body bows in a graceful arch and then extends back to the teacher's (a touch optimistic, one might think) exhortation to 'touch the ceiling'. A dancer uses the whole body – rather like a young infant just learning to feed himself. All the limbs, the head and torso are brought into action.

The language of the moves is French, but the pronunciation is not necessarily that to be found in Paris. But do not worry, there is a special section where we concentrate on this. There is no need to worry anyway – such workshops are very informal affairs. The measure of this is that the children laugh and play and are not nearly so well-behaved (or frightened?) as they are in a surgical outpatient department at the hospital!

When a period of exercise is done in the military then the muscles are relaxed afterwards in a series of stretches. It is quite funny to see that when soldiers have to stand on one leg they hop about like crazy break-dancers. Even young children in ballet 'workshops' seem to be able to manage this without holding onto their neighbour for balance. Perhaps only those with good natural poise turn up.

For those of our readers who can remember the introduction where we wrote about spinning to the right or left, and which is easier or preferable, the teacher ensures that in her 'workshop' that any movement or dance sequence is repeated in the opposite direction 'just to even ourselves up'.

Those left behind

JB had the great pleasure of making the acquaintance of a good-looking psychologist who was exceptionally well proportioned and athletic. No, it wasn't that sort of psychologist holding a group session:

> Hello, I'm John, I'm a greedy fat bastard who cannot stop eating.

Welcome John, group hug etc., or whatever they have at Weight Watchers Anonymous. She is Professor of Psychology at the University of Seville. First Thursday of the month is devoted to making Rorschach ink patches and she was busy scrubbing her hands clean. I was there inspecting oranges for the Medical School at which I was working. In the medical world they are used for novices to practice injections. Funnily enough, hairdressers do not make use of coconuts to practise their first haircuts, which seems a mistake. Anyway, back to the point. In order to fully research this book, I often quiz attractive women on whether they attended ballet classes when young. I was absolutely amazed, as a medical man, to hear that as a child she had suffered from knee problems and had been forbidden sport. At times she had even had difficulty managing stairs, let alone dancing. There are a variety of developmental orthopaedic problems such as this, thankfully uncommon, and often, as in her case, with no long-lasting consequences. At the time, she had felt very much left out of things. Peer pressure drives us to conform and we feel excluded if we cannot – it is natural to want to join in and feel part of the crowd. The reader is referred to our Introduction and JB's experiences as a schoolchild. These were repeated (almost) when on a recent language course. At mealtimes two Spaniards had to sit with two English to further their conversational abilities. There was a definite tenseness as one sat at an empty table, willing someone to come and sit down. But not him. Why not her? And if she comes, would she bring her friend? It was the school playground all over again. As is much of life. How true it has been said that a school is a jail with educational opportunities – and the added economic duty of keeping the able-bodied away from the labour market. It might be said of ballet school that one learns how to bend but not break – but this time literally!

Ballet or some form of dance may, though, have the ability to allow children otherwise excluded from physical activities to take part. Children do seem a little fickle – they often enjoy physical exercise, but it has to be presented in the right way. In an article by Niki Cardwell in *BBC News* (15 September 2007) entitled 'Computer dance gets pupils active' it seems that even young people who hate sport will take exercise. *Dance Revolution* involves laying out removable mats in a studio, and getting participants to follow instructions from a computer on a large screen. Each mat transmits how well each pupil is doing and the results are flashed up on the screen. Despite this, one of the attractions seems to be, according to one of the pupils:

> If you make a mistake, no-one notices because they are doing their own thing and you can catch up.

The classes are being targeted at girls in Bedfordshire who are not interested in traditional sports. Daniel Gill, of *Active Luton*, the trust which runs local sports and leisure facilities, said:

> *You tend to burn about 400 to 600 calories an hour in these classes. You are working on coordination, balance, cardio vascular, stamina. Each class lasts for 45 minutes and the programme allows you to choose from five levels of difficulty. There is no segregation on ability. Even if they know they can't do all of it, they can try anyway. And it's a good way of introducing them to a gym.*

The head of physical education noted that there were students 'who we don't reach with competitive sports'. The trial classes proved so popular that they have now been opened up to all pupils as part of Lea Manor's sports curriculum and as an after school activity. Daniel Gill said:

> *This is not just for kids, adults use it as well. In the public sessions we have been getting whole families coming in. How many sports out there can you think of that work for the whole family?*

It might also be found that doing something one enjoys rather than is forced to do can work wonders for health. A child might willingly go to an enjoyable dance class but 'be too poorly for school'.

In an article which (amongst other things) touched on the problem of why Britain seems to be producing fewer of the dancers than it should be, the question was raised as to allocation of resources. Should more money be put into 'ordinary' schools at the expense of specialist schools such as The Royal Ballet Junior School? Attendance there requires an earlier commitment, but of course has the advantage that resources are concentrated. There is the chance to work with the Company (in roles where children are required) and members of the Company give solo classes and extra help – though mostly for the Upper School. In fact, students at the Upper School of The Royal Ballet sometimes have the opportunity to work with the Company, a situation which was once reported as:

> *'They are being forced to do this at the moment for* Swan Lake *as there have been so many injuries'.*

Class

No writing by British authors would be complete without some mention of class – not acting/dancing or school classes, but social class. It is a popular belief that ballet is somewhat upper class – the people who watch it and those who send their children to ballet classes. Amongst the wealthy, this might be seen almost as a rite of passage. Were this not the case, then why did the film *Billy Elliot* make such a splash? There are, of course, many exceptions, and the last thing our publishers want is a torrent of correspondence pointing out how readers do not fall into this generalisation. But that is what it is – a generalisation – a commonly held feeling that in private schools ballet is likely to be offered as an option, better off parents seek out classes for their children, and in poorer communities ballet is far less likely to be found. Of course, this can sometimes prove to be a difficulty, as was related to JB by a woman who as a young girl had participated in both the required activities for young ladies: ballet and horse-riding. The equestrians wanted her to push in her knees, toes in, ankles out etc – the ballet mistress quite the opposite. She managed to succeed in neither. Another of the perils of wealth! There are compensations, though. Even at a young age JB realised that Father Christmas seemed to favour the children of more affluent families.

This is a subject which is always guaranteed to add some sparkle to a boring dinner party and it is amazing what heat can be generated by supporters and refuters of the above general statements. The 'aspirational' element of ballet was brought home to JB recently by someone who works in the field of advertising – Arantza. Those who know him will wonder what advertising circles JB moves in. Why, apart from a brief spell holding the paste bucket for a bill sticker (a holiday job he acquired after experience as a wringer-out for a one-armed window cleaner), surely he knows nothing? Well, not quite nothing. Did you know, for example, that those large pillars in German streets whose sole purpose is to hold adverts are called Litfaßsäule named after their inventor Dr Ernst Litfass, a German printer and publisher? Exactly.

Well, Arantza is the acceptable face of capitalism and advertising, and a remarkably bright and good-looking woman to boot. She acts as the intermediary between two groups. On the one side the money men with their budgets, target audience, sales profiles, yields and returns. On the other, the pony-tailed, double decaff skinny latte, designer stubble creative types. OK, we are stereotyping a bit. Anyway, the money men wanted to 'increase the exposure' of their cell phones and the talk plans which went with them. The arty types needed to emphasise the cost-saving and value – but to pitch it at a higher creative level than the 'pile them high, sell them cheap' ethos of the supermarket, they came up with a plan. This was to emphasise that with the money saved, a family could then afford the important, finer things in life – such as ballet lessons for the children. The advert was shot at a ballet school. By gosh, these creative types certainly earn their millions!

So there we have it – ballet is an aspirational activity (as the ponytails say). This was also no doubt the feeling of *Family Guy* writer Patrick Meighan when he has Peter Griffin dress up and go to the ballet (*Family Guy,* 20th Century Fox Film Corporation Episode SACXll). Downcast, he obliges the family, but cheers up when he meets Quagmire there (who is with a girl he is 'trying to nail') and they start texting each other across the balcony. It is clear that ballet is a 'sophisticated' event – one dresses up and it is not for 'macho' men – unless they are trying to impress a woman.

Whilst speaking of class, the following cautionary tale is probably in order. The first floor of Au Printemps (Maison de la Mode) is named 'luxe' and is where the really expensive brands are to be found – Chanel, Cartier, Hermès and the like. The toilets are similarly luxurious – more tastefully painted and more spacious. But they are not as clean as on other floors and more likely to be out of order. The reason? People who don't really belong on the luxury floor (like your authors) WANT TO USE THEM. Aim a little lower, and you end up being better off. Philosophical authors might wax lyrical for several paragraphs on this theme. We will not.

The reader should note, however, how costs can sometimes work doubly for an organisation. The sale price is high so the profit is increased, and because it costs a lot it is 'exclusive' and hence sought after. This is shown by coffee houses. In Manchester city centre there is a well-known 'exclusive' chain of coffee shops. The branch there sells coffee to take away for more than double the price of the bakery a few doors down. It is more expensive than the branch of a much smaller and less posh chain at the end of the street – which had to close down. Perhaps the quality is just so fantastic that people will pay a premium? Well they certainly do pay more, but whether for quality or the cachet of the name is not certain. JB went in for a 'fresh orange juice'. It came in a plastic bottle with the words 'lightly pasteurised'. Pasteurisation is a process of sterilisation by heating to a high temperature; if the temperature is not high then it is not pasteurised.

To finish off something about class, what could be more indicative than the feel of the need to hide one's origins. Why a name change? What is in a name? Lauren Cuthbertson was advised to do so but after considering various possibilities decided to stick with what was on her birth certificate – with no ill effect. However, Edris Stannus transformed herself into Ninette de Valois, Peggy Hookham felt that her chances would be better as Margot Fonteyn and Cyvian Rambam became better known as Marie Rambert, founder of Ballet Rambert.

Other forms of dance – including Irish dancing!!

The television documentary *Ballrooms and Ballerinas* (BBC4 23 January 2022) does not confine itself to ballet, and neither will this book! Ballroom dancing played a large role in dance in the 20th century. The BBC became more of a national service after the Second World War – pre-war television sets were very rare and mostly confined to London, though of course it was the

Coronation of 1953 which really increased their number. 1948 saw the introduction of *Television Dancing Club*, hosted by Victor Sylvester. He had started his career being a ballroom dancing partner for guests at Harrods' Georgian restaurant – at a salary of £1 per week. The ballroom was the main place to find romance and it is said that it was there that 75% of married couples first met. It was, however, essentially pre-war entertainment and by the mid-1950s was being seen as increasingly middle-aged. By the end of the 1960s the expectation of romance and marriage was moving away from the dance floor. Dance was less about romantic dancing together and more a means of free expression, in line with the increasing permissiveness of society. On television, dance troupes appeared – this was in the days before music videos so it allowed shows such as Top of the Pops to play records when the bands were not available. The best known was *Pan's People*, later to be replaced by the more provocative, skimpily dressed *Hot Gossip*.

Irish dancing for me

We now have a little insert entitled 'Irish dancing for me' – to give that further international flavour which has so beguiled critics at the book festivals to which this work has been invited. This woman no longer dances, but has fond recollections of her girlhood in Northern Ireland. In fact, whenever *Lord of the Dance* is played, her toes start tapping. Your authors have not personally verified this, but have no reason to doubt the accuracy of the statement. We just don't want to have to play *Lord of the Dance*!

At primary school she would skip around the playground with arms firmly at her side. There is a theory that the original peat bog where the ancient manuscripts describing Irish dances were found failed to give up the chapters referring to 'what to do with the hands'. She was terrified to pause to scratch her nose or lose her step. But why such discipline? Tradition dictated that they follow their Irish heritage in both music and dance. Here we find subtle differences between the Republic of Ireland, where the dresses were velvet and the North, where silk was worn, often with a sash. Neither group would appear on the same stage, or wear the same colours. They agreed on the footwear, though; to begin with there is a slipper similar to ballet. Later as the girl progresses this is reinforced at the toe so that she can pivot. Finally (by the age of about twelve) a proper Irish dancing shoe is worn.

For her, the dancing classes were something to be endured, rather than enjoyed. This was probably the result of a rather mean-spirited teacher who had missed the point that dancing is meant to be fun. We have heard similar experiences from former schoolchildren (modern idiom: schoolkids) and their Latin classes. Despite her early experiences, she maintains a pride in her cultural heritage and the spirit of the dance lives on for her. Sadly, the same cannot often be said for Latin, which is rarely used and often forgotten. You disagree?

What are the principal parts of 'facere', then? You think you know, but you don't.

Famous Ballets

Including:

- **Classical ballets**
- **More modern ballets**
- **Ballet and celebrity**
- **Ballet and diversity**
- **Ballet companies and their stages**
- **A short history of fashion and the arts**

Followed by an INTERMISSION!

CLASSICAL BALLETS

The Nutcracker
Swan Lake
The Sleeping Beauty
Aurora's Wedding
Don Quixote
Cinderella
Romeo and Juliet
The Dream
Coppélia
Giselle
Bayadère

DIAGHILEV BALLETS

Petrushka
L'Après-midi d'un Faune
Le Sacre du Printemps / The Rite of Spring
Les Noces
Les Biches

MORE MODERN BALLETS

Sanguine Fan
Gaîté Parisienne
Nutcracker 'Spin-offs'
Carmen
Salome
The Golden Age
Jewels
Song of the Earth
The Snow Queen
Seven Deadly Sins
Checkmate
Symphonic Variations
Queen of Spades
Isadora
Les Patineurs

BALLETS BASED ON OTHER SOURCES

Ballet based on art
Train Bleu
Tricorne
Rake
Miss Carter
A Simple Man

Ballet based on music
Les Sylphides
Pineapple Poll
Fancy Free
Parade
Enigma
Rooster
Satisfaction
Billboards
Nine Sinatra Songs
Elite Syncopations

Ballet based on poetry
Ballet and animals
Ballet and celebrity
Ballet and diversity

BALLET COMPANIES AND THEIR STAGES
ROH and Covent Garden
Royal Ballet
Birmingham Royal Ballet
Sadler's Wells

FAMOUS NAMES IN BALLET AND THE ARTS

A SHORT HISTORY OF FASHION AND THE ARTS
(inc. some technological developments!)

Followed by an INTERMISSION!

It is not always necessary to know the intricacies of the story which a ballet portrays, and nobody should feel diminished if they do not. The reader may be surprised to learn that in opera only a proportion (it can be lower than fifty per cent) of the words of the dialogue are recognised by the audience. Nevertheless, an idea of what is going on can be helpful. The programme notes, which are usually only available at the performance itself, will give an outline. This is invariably a satisfactory synopsis of the plot. What follows in this section does in no way attempt to compete, but the advantage lies in that you have the notes here at home (or wherever this book is being read). For those who find abstract dance a little difficult or baffling, you are not alone in preferring something with a story. In an interview (*Daily Telegraph* 11 July 2015) a dancer named 'the hottest ticket in dance', Ivan Vasiliev, held that for him, 'ballets without a story are always a little bit difficult'. He considers that it is a problem when he does not understand what is to be said to the audience: 'I must just dance – but for what?'

So this chapter does not contain slavishly reproduced summaries of the plots of every ballet ever made – there are encyclopaedia-like reference books already devoted to this subject. As an example, we can suggest the two volume Balanchine work devoted solely to this topic (though there is nothing whatsoever about *The Sanguine Fan*!). It may be found in your local library and each volume is about the size of a telephone directory (for those who remember such things!). The library JB visits has no ballet books (subsection 792.8) on its shelves, though does keep some old ones in the stacks, available on personal request. In contrast, Norse Sagas (subsection 870) contains two books! In summary, as promised in the title of this book, we give you The Interesting Stuff!

Classical Ballets

The Nutcracker

Almost as much a part of Christmas as Santa Claus himself, this was Tchaikovsky's final ballet. He was apparently not too happy with it, but it is probably the second most famous ballet of all. The reasons for this, and just where it is popular, are surprisingly controversial. In a remarkable demonstration of how simple innocent pleasures such as ballet can be utilised for political purposes, an assistant professor of dance history and theory wrote on the Americanisation (and hence improvement!) of *The Nutcracker* (*New York Times* Op-Ed Opinion 13 Dec 2003). She began with the theory that it is not a Russian ballet anymore, but a North American phenomenon. She considers that although first presented in imperial St Petersburg in 1892, 'it never really blossomed there'... 'it didn't catch on in Europe either'. *The Nutcracker* went to the USA, first to San Francisco in 1944, arriving in New York some ten years later, with George Balanchine giving it 'a sparkling new look, with lots of special effects and new choreography'. The answer in its success probably lies outside Balanchine's undoubted genius:

> First, for many companies the annual Christmas *Nutcracker* can 'bankroll an entire season' (the professor's words).

> Second, transatlantic choreographers have adapted the settings to make it look more like their own communities, adding hula in Hawaii, hockey in Winnipeg, and skateboarding in inner-city versions.

Add to that the opportunities for local ballet schools to send their students to actually take part in the performance, and you have a winning combination. When it first opened in 1892, it came as half of a Tchaikovsky double bill; the other half was the 84-minute *Iolanta,* a story in which adult love cures the heroine's blindness.

Swan Lake

This was Tchaikovsky's first ballet (1876) and is probably the most famous of all. As we have just read (v.s.) his last was the second most famous. So what was he doing in between? We have a short section on composers and the arts in general later on. Not too much. Just enough. The sort of thing that, having read it, one can avoid unpleasantness at dinner parties, concert intervals etc. Put people in their place – you know the drill by now. We will see you right. Anyway, *Swan Lake* is based on the German legend of Prince Siegfried who falls in love with Odette. No problems there, you might think, but Odette is a princess under the spell of the evil Rothbart. She is a woman only by night – the rest of the time she is a swan. Rothbart tricks Siegfried into betraying her. There are various versions of the ending – the best has the two tragic lovers dying together in the lake, destroying Rothbart in the process. It is said that Stalin did not like this non-optimistic conclusion so it was altered for the Soviet audience!

The Sleeping Beauty

The Sleeping Beauty is a timeless ballet which has been constantly popular since its first performance at the Mariinsky Theatre, St Petersburg on 13 January 1890 when Marius Petipa was at the peak of his career. At that time the fashion was for spectacular fairy ballets and the idea of basing one on the famous fairy tale, *La Belle au Bois Dormant,* by Charles Perrault was by no means unusual.

Tchaikovsky was chosen to write the music. Thirty years later the ballet still survived in a changed world – the Tsar was gone and St Petersburg now had the name of Petrograd, but regular performances still took place. In 1921 Diaghilev had the inspiration of showing London the glories of the Imperial Ballet by reviving the same *Sleeping Beauty*, but renamed *The Sleeping Princess*. Although it ran for 105 performances, this was not enough to recoup the enormous expenditure, and the scenery was impounded for the debt. Diaghilev was never able to stage the complete ballet again, but some of the designs and costumes survived to be sold as works of art in their own right in 1968. *The Sleeping Beauty* has since been restaged all over the world and was the ballet chosen by the then Sadler's Wells Ballet to reopen Covent Garden in 1946. Such fame and popularity can count against it – in an interview broadcast by the BBC, Deborah Bull pointed out that when the Royal Opera House was short of money (which seems a lot of the time), then artistic adventurousness tends to be curbed. Safety becomes the order of the day and 'things like another *Sleeping Beauty* brought out'. Still, this seems to be what people want. See the section on 'Ballet and Celebrity' later on in this chapter.

Aurora's Wedding

This is a version of the last act with many fairytale characters coming to the wedding celebrations of Princess Aurora and Prince Florimund, including the Blue Birds, White Cat, Puss-in-Boots and all the fairies. Sometimes well-known parts of the full ballet are incorporated. When staged by Peter Wright for The Royal Ballet, he had the well-known pas d'action from the prologue and the final act's divertissements to give an opportunity for a magnificent display of classical dancing.

Don Quixote

Music: Minkus Choreography: Petipa

Based on the novel by Miguel Cervantes, this has a ballet history dating back to the mid-nineteenth century with Petipa's version first presented by the Bolshoi Ballet Theatre in 1869. In 1966 the Bolshoi performed a revised version in the USA by Gorsky and Zakharov. The barber Basil is in love with the innkeeper's daughter Kitri, but her father wants her to marry an effete nobleman, Gamche. Don Quixote, with his manservant Sancho Panza, arrives at the inn, mistaking it for a castle. He thinks that Kitri is his lost love Dulcinea and is transported into a dreamworld where she appears in many guises. Finally he realises what has happened and that Kitri and Basil should marry.

Cinderella

Music: Prokofiev   Choreography: Valery Panov
Matthew Bourne famously recreated this, setting it during the London Blitz of 1940.

Cinderella is made to perform chores by her stepmother and two stepsisters who scold and taunt her. They, however, have been invited by the prince to a grand ball at the castle, leaving Cinderella alone and sad. A beggar woman arrives to be rebuffed by the three of them and it is only Cinderella who, unobserved, provides her with food and clothing. Cinderella falls asleep and dreams of the ball. The beggar appears, changes into a shining fairy and provides her with a suitable dress and servants to go to the ball, but she must leave at midnight. She departs in such a hurry and is restored to her former wretched state, leaving only a slipper. The prince tries to track her down by having everybody try it on – it fits nobody. Finally he finds the family home where he is reunited with Cinderella and all, in true tradition, live happily ever after.

Romeo and Juliet

Music: Prokofiev   Choreography: Psota
Set by many of the world's greatest choreographers, including Anthony Tudor, Frederick Ashton and Kenneth MacMillan (whose production starred Margot Fonteyn and Rudolf Nureyev).

Sergey Prokofiev's score underwent many changes before arriving at the version used today. He had written music for a ballet with a happy ending, because, in his words 'living people can dance, the dying cannot'. After much debate with his colleagues the music was changed to express the tragic ending Shakespeare had intended. This was not to Stalin's liking so the version seen in the Soviet Union reverted to a happy ending.

The Dream
Music: Felix Mendelssohn   Choreography: Frederick Ashton

Following a quarrel between the king and queen of the fairies the king anoints the queen's eyes with a magic herb that will make her fall in love with the first creature she sees. This happens to be a peasant who has been transformed into a donkey. Meanwhile two lovers arrive, followed by a man to whom one has been promised by her father. The king once again tries his magic potion but it ends up in the wrong eyes and confusion abounds…

Coppélia
Music: Delibes   Choreography: Arthur Michel Saint Léon

The plot was taken from Hoffman's story *Der Sandmann,* which introduced the world of automatons, dolls and marionettes. A life-sized puppet, Coppélia, has been constructed by Dr Coppelius for his travelling puppet theatre. It is seen by Franz and Swanilda, who are to become engaged, and is so lifelike that Swanilda tries to talk to it. Franz flirts with the puppet, making Swanilda jealous. Dr Coppelius invites Franz to his caravan and drugs him in an attempt to transfer his spirit to Coppélia. But Swanilda has changed places with Coppélia with predictable results as confusion ensues.

Giselle
Music: Adolphe Adam   Choreography: Marius Petipa after Jean Coralli and Jules Perrot

This most celebrated ballet of the Romantic era owes its creation to the French poet Théophile Gautier who had been inspired by the German legend of the Wilis which he had found in a poem by Heine. He devised a ballet scenario for the Paris Opéra with Adolphe Adam being commissioned to write the music (which he completed in little more than a week!) and ballet master Jean Coralli the choreography – but the title role Giselle was choreographed by her husband, Jules Perrot.

Giselle, a peasant girl, is loved by Count Albrecht – although she only knows him as the villager, Loys. Gisele's mother hopes that she will marry a forester (Hilarion) who is devoted to Giselle, but she spurns him. Hilarion breaks into Loys' cottage trying to find his true identity. He succeeds in this, and to compound Giselle's problems, Albrecht's future bride, a duke's daughter, arrives. Giselle dies and a vigil is kept by Hilarion at her grave. At midnight the Wilis materialise – ghosts of young girls jilted and dead before their wedding day, who avenge themselves by dancing to death any man they meet during the hours of darkness. Hilarion is driven to his death but Albrecht is saved by the arrival of daybreak when the Wilis and Giselle melt away, leaving him alone and sorrowful. Not exactly a Hollywood happy ending!

La Bayadère
Music: Minkus Choreography: Petipa

This is a full-length 19th-century ballet classic of love, murder and vengeful judgement by the gods. In order that the story line does not become too confused with Coronation St, it is set in the India of the Romantic imagination. The noble warrior Solor returns from a tiger hunt. In secret he has sworn eternal love to Nikiya, a bayadère (temple dancer). But the High Brahmin is also in love with her, although she has rejected him and when he spies on the two of them together it only enflames his jealousy. Meanwhile the Rajah has decided his daughter Gamzatti will marry Solor. When she meets him, her great beauty makes the warrior forget Nikiya and his vows of love. So far, pretty much the standard nineteenth century ballet fare, one might think. But wait, things get nasty. The rejected High Brahmin does not go for counselling or out with his mates to get drunk. Instead, he tells the Rajah of Nikiya and Solor's love, hoping this will get Solor executed. A cunning plan – but instead the Rajah demands Nikiya's death. Nikiya refuses to dance at the celebrations to mark the impending marriage of Gamzatti and Solor, but brightens up when told a basket of flowers presented to her is from Solor. In fact the gift is from the Rajah and Gamzatti. A snake has been hidden in it. This bites Nikiya, killing her. In despair, Solor resorts to opium, which induces a beautiful vision of multiple Nikiyas in the spirit world. Later, at the wedding ceremony in the temple, Solor is again haunted by the vision of Nikiya which he alone can see. Despite the High Brahmin's attempts to perform the marriage ceremony, Solor refuses to say his vows. The gods, infuriated by Nikiya's murder, destroy the temple, killing everyone in it. In a final image, the spirits of Nikiya and Solor are seen reunited in eternal love in the next world.

Diaghilev ballets

Petrushka

Music: Stravinsky   Choreography: Fokine

This one-act ballet, divided into four scenes, was completed and staged by the Ballets Russes at the Théâtre du Châtelet in Paris 1911. A magician has three puppets: Petrushka and the Moor, who fight over the third – the Ballerina. The Magician has endowed his puppets with human feelings, but this throws Petrushka into despair as he longs for a human existence to match his human desires. The Moor seduces the Ballerina but is interrupted by Petrushka, who is slain dead by him. The stunned onlookers are convinced by the Magician that Petrushka is only a puppet made of wood and straw and disperse, but after this the Magician sees the ghost of Petrushka threatening him.

L'Après-midi d'un Faune

Music: Debussy   Choreography: Vaslav Nijinsky

This was Nijinsky's first work as a choreographer (1912), with he himself dancing the faune. He distances himself from the then accepted traditions of ballet, using a two-dimensional concept, with simple gestures and postures, suggestive of the figures on classic Greek vase paintings. Seven nymphs pass by a faune who is playing the flute on their way to bathe in a nearby lake. He is entranced by their beauty and they in turn are fascinated by him. One remains, but eventually takes fright and rushes off to join her companions, leaving a silk scarf. The faune, sad at her departure, caresses it, imagining it to be her and returns contentedly to his hillside, dreaming of the nymphs.

Le Sacre du Printemps / The Rite of Spring
Music: Igor Stravinsky Choreography: Vaslav Nijinsky

The first reaction at the Paris premiere was perhaps the most violent in 20th century art, with the audience alternately jeering, booing and applauding. Subtitled as *Pictures of Pagan Russia,* this describes how, according to Russian legend, a young girl was ritually chosen each year to dance herself to death. By doing so the energies of spring were released from the frozen earth.

Les Noces
Music: Stravinsky Choreography: Bronislava Nijinska

This ballet in four scenes depicts a Russian peasant wedding at the beginning of the Christian era in Russia when pagan rituals were still retained as family traditions. The four choreographic scenes were composed between 1914 and 1923 and first presented in Paris in 1923 by Diaghilev's Ballets Russes.

Les Biches
Music: Poulenc Choreography: Bronislava Nijinska

Set in the south of France at a privileged house party of the 1920s, this comprises eight dance numbers with slight jazz accents. Three handsome boys flirt and parade their muscles before the hostess and a group of giggling girls. 'La Biche' is colloquial French for a little darling, but clearly has potential for being misunderstood!

Jane Howarth (English National Ballet artistic coordinator) wrote that ballet has regressed from Diaghilev's day (*Diaghilev's Ballets Russes 100 years, The Times* 2 May 2009) holding that:

> *'it is all about the safe option now – you cannot be as creative as you want artistically'.*

Diaghilev would be shocked by how conservative ballet is in the age of publicly funded organisations. He knew what it meant to scrabble for money, with his company often on the brink of financial collapse.

An uncertain financial position did not prevent him from seeking to provoke and amaze his audiences with the shock of the new. The concept of one-act ballets upon which Ballets Russes was based is now hard to sell at the box office, with companies tending to rely on popular full-length productions. These are just the sort that Diaghilev had left behind, although he did stage *The Sleeping Beauty* (or *The Sleeping Princess,* as he called it) in London 1921.

As a further service to readers of this book it should be noted that the best person to borrow money from is a pessimist – who probably will never expect to get it back.

More modern ballets

The Sanguine Fan
Music: Elgar Choreography: Hynd

The music for this piece was written specially by Sir Edward Elgar – the only score he wrote specifically for ballet. Later, some of his music has of course been used for ballet, most notably the *Enigma Variations.* This was a special commission in 1917 for a matinée in aid of war charities. It was inspired by a fan on which the artist Charles Conder had drawn the mythological characters Pan and Echo in a grove with young men and women wearing eighteenth century clothes. The premiere was at the Chelsea Palace in March 1917 with a second performance in May for which Elgar added a shepherd's dance. One wonders just how much money was actually made for the charities with so much effort going into just two performances! Extracts from the music were recorded three years later with the composer conducting, but after that the score seems to have been forgotten.

It was not until 1973 that Sir Adrian Boult made a recording of it with the London Philharmonic Orchestra, and suggested to Sir Frederick Ashton that he make a ballet to it. Ashton thought it too soon after his *Enigma Variations*, as did Ronald Hynd. Hynd did, however, keep the music in mind and, when he was asked to create a work for London Festival Ballet to perform at the Seventh Monte Carlo International Arts Festival, decided to use it. The result was *L'Éventail*, and it received its premiere in Monte Carlo on 10 July 1976. JB saw it in Manchester performed by the same company on 11 March 1977 and still has the programme (cost 10p!).

Hynd and his designer Peter Docherty altered the original considerably and drew greatly upon Oscar Wilde's play, *Lady Windermere's Fan*. The action takes place in 1905 in a large London house overlooking a park. A party is hosted by twin brothers who are both infatuated by the same woman. Choices have to be made and misunderstandings set right. A fan is lost, along with tempers. The moral might be not to judge by appearances, but prose does not adequately describe the ballet which set JB off on his love of the art. To avoid disappointment it should be perhaps pointed out to some (emphasis some) of our American readers that there is no car chase or multiple shootings.

Gaîté Parisienne

Music: Offenbach Choreography: Massine

This delightful ballet, which formed the third of the trio of ballets first seen by JB (see 'The First Ballet I Ever Saw'), was first produced in Monte Carlo in 1938 by the newly formed Ballet Russe de Monte Carlo. Comte Etienne de Beaumont, a highly creative dilettante, had had the idea of a ballet to music by Offenbach ever since acquiring the scores of over a hundred Offenbach operettas.

Working with his old friend and collaborator, Leonide Massine, the scene was set in a popular café, Tortonis.

The action centres around a Charlie Chaplin-like character who bounds on the stage with two carpet bags of jewels he is seeking to sell and then conquer Paris. There are various subplots – an Austrian baron and an officer vie for an attractive glove seller and the stage is filled with colourful figures of the French Second Empire to which Offenbach's music, arranged by Manuel Rosenthal, fits perfectly.

Nutcracker 'Spin-offs'
We might as well put these in at this point whilst the reader's mind is still fresh from what we wrote about the classical *Nutcracker.* The story lends itself to further adaptation, especially with a populist theme, as shown by the following:

Nutcracker Sweeties
Music: Duke Ellington Choreography. David Bintley

Billy Strayhorn and Duke Ellington's big band take on Tchaikovsky by portraying Broadway in the 1940s. The dancers are dressed in glamorous Jasper Conran costumes – pom pom girls, drum majorettes, sailors, GIs and Candy Cane.

The Hard Nut
Music: Tchaikovsky Choreography: Mark Morris

This is based, like the more conventional *Nutcracker,* on the original story by ETA Hoffman, but differs in that the scary parts are left in. The idea for this came from the comics artist Charles Burns and is not the cosy nineteenth century but the world of the 1960s and 1970s. The story begins conventionally enough but then develops overtones of *Cinderella.* In the second act the family friend Drosselmeier (who had brought the nutcracker) is telling Marie the story of a baby princess who is bitten by a rat and cursed to be ugly. This spell can only be lifted by a magic nut being cracked by a young man's teeth. The inevitable happens

– Drosselmeier's handsome young nephew succeeds, but in his attempt, steps on the rat queen, transferring the spell to himself. At this point Marie interrupts Drosselmeier's story and offers her own love to his nephew. In other words, you can search all over for love, but end up finding it on your doorstep.

Carmen

Music: Rodion Shchedrin Choreography: Alberto Alonsin based on the novel by Mérimée

This is one of the many examples of ballet derived from opera. It was first choreographed for Maya Plisetskaya with the Bolshoi Ballet and first performed in Cuba. The story is the familiar one of Carmen, free and true to herself, falling in love with Don José and then leaving him for the glamorous toreador. This takes place in a simulated bullring, emphasising the character of the participants rather than the plot. The final pas de deux is a dance contest between Carmen and Don José and takes the form of a simulated bull fight. The ballerina assumes the combined roles of heroine and fate in the form of a bull.

Salome

Music: Richard Strauss Choreography: Various

Salome was the third opera written by Richard Strauss. It was completed in 1905, receiving its first performance in Dresden where the audience found it shocking due to its extremes of emotion. The libretto was from a German translation of the verse drama by Oscar Wilde and tells the story of how the stepdaughter of King Herod brings about the death of John the Baptist. She dances the dance of seven veils and is asked to name her reward – she chooses his head on a silver platter.

The Golden Age

Music: Shostakovich Choreography: Grigorovich

Set in the roaring twenties, this revolves around 'The Golden Age' nightclub and highlights some of the ideological issues of the post-revolutionary period. The decadent bourgeoisie clash with the young fishermen, who are all members of the Young Workers' Propaganda Theatre. It would be churlish to spoil the end, but not much got past Stalin, if that is a clue. For the reader too inpatient to wait to see the ballet, a more detailed explanation is given later in the section on political associations and ballet.

Jewels
Music: Various Choreography: Balanchine

This is a three-part ballet, and possibly the first ever full-length abstract work. It was inspired by a visit made by Balanchine to a Manhattan jeweller and encompasses three different dance eras:

> Emeralds – the earliest Romantic French ballet – set to the music of Gabriel Fauré
>
> Rubies – an American work inspired by jazz and syncopation and set to Stravinsky
>
> Diamonds – Russian with a full ensemble in tutus dancing to Tchaikovsky.

Song of the Earth
Music: Gustav Mahler Choreography: Kenneth MacMillan

This ballet is based on Mahler's music composed when he knew he was dying from an incurable heart condition. It is based on a book of eighth century Chinese poems about the transience of life. A man, woman and the messenger of death dance to six songs sung by a tenor and mezzo soprano.

The Snow Queen
Music: Prokofiev Choreography: Michael Corder

This is billed as 'freely adapted from the fairy tale by Hans Christian Anderson' (as is *Stories From A Flying Trunk*) and tells the tale of two young friends, Kay (who is the boy) and Gerda. Kay catches slivers of the Snow Queen's shattered magic mirror in his eye and heart and is spirited away to her palace. Eternal winter descends on the village. Gerda searches worldwide for her lost friend on a journey which finally brings her to him at the palace. Her love for Kay releases him from the spell and the Snow Queen's curse of eternal winter is lifted.

The Seven Deadly Sins

Music: Weill Libretto: Brecht Choreography: Tuckett

This received its premiere in Paris, June 1933 as a 'sung ballet' by Kurt Weill and Bertolt Brecht. Brecht had fled Germany four months before, the day after the Reichstag fire. Three weeks later Weill, whose new play Die Silbersee had closed by Nazi edict, being denounced as mindless, inferior and sick, also left Berlin for Paris. The piece uses a singer and a dancer to portray two sides of the same woman as she journeys across the USA to earn money to support her family in Louisiana. It was conceived as a vicious satire on American greed and with each city she visits she encounters a new sin, becoming more and more corrupted in the process.

Kurt Weill composed the music in less than a month.

Checkmate

Music: Arthur Bliss Choreography: Ninette de Valois

First performed in 1937, this is a cruel fantasy – a battle of life and death acted out as a game of chess. There is another level, though – in the time leading up to the Second World War it had overtones of the coming conflict. The Black Queen may be seen as representing Hitler, and the red pawns the mind of the masses, easily influenced by external events. It begins with two players, who disclose themselves as Love and Death, fighting for the lives of their subjects. The leading role is given to a ballerina rather than to the male dancer and is another example of how de Valois tried to produce ballets that sprung directly from English sources with some parts having their roots in the English folk dance tradition of Morris dancing. She also used native English talent for both the score and the designs.

Symphonic Variations
Music: César Franck   Choreography: Sir Frederick Ashton

Sir Frederick had listened to Franck's music throughout the Second World War and vowed to choreograph a piece celebrating peace and calm to his work. The dancers are on stage for a full twenty minutes with no let-up in a series of technically demanding demonstrations of pure ballet technique to the accompaniment of an orchestra and solo piano.

Queen of Spades
Music: Prokofiev   Choreography: Brandstrup

The Russian composer Sergei Prokofiev was commissioned in 1936 to write the score for a film which was cancelled. The lost score was found by the Danish choreographer Kim Brandstrup who contacted The Royal Ballet, as he believed it could be turned into a dance piece. At first the Prokofiev estate was wary about this plan not only to combine some pieces of unfinished music into a complete work but then also to adapt it to another medium. Their fears were unjustified and the work *The Queen of Spades* was performed as a ballet at Covent Garden.

Isadora
Music: Richard Rodney Bennett   Choreography: MacMillan

Created by Kenneth MacMillan in 1981, this ballet commemorates the American dancer Isadora Duncan and was revived in a shortened form in 2009 for The Royal Ballet, being cut by an hour from the original two hours twenty minutes. She was a larger than life character, scandalising society with several high profile love affairs, losing her two children in a Parisian drowning accident in 1913, and dying from her scarf being caught in the wheel of a sports car in Nice fourteen years later. She pioneered the free dance movement, leading to dancers everywhere replacing tutus with tunics, kaftans etc. and rediscovering nature. It is a 'revolution' which has a recurring theme through the decades!

Every so often there are reports that ballet is experiencing a renaissance. Often these prove to be premature. In 2010 *The Observer* (5 December 2010) reported 'ballet is bursting with vitality, spilling beyond the doors of its traditional homes'. This was prompted by the announcement that Carlos Acosta and Tamara Rojo would be performing on the stage of the O2 arena the following year. As well as this, the *Pet Shop Boys* were to score a ballet with Venezuelan choreographer Javier De Frutos, Emily Blunt would appear as a member of a ballet troop in the film *Adjustment Bureau* and Natalie Portman star in *Black Swan*. A decade on, ballet is very much alive but hardly to the extent so optimistically predicted.

***Les Patineurs* (Skaters)**
Music: Meyerbeer Choreography: Ashton

This charming skating divertissement uses the flowing rhythms of Meyerbeer's score to evoke the movements of skaters of all proficiency, from the expert teacher to the most inexpert of beginners. Work was originally started by Ninette de Valois in an arrangement by Constant Lambert, but she found herself unable to make much progress. Frederick Ashton had heard the music in rehearsal and admired it so much he needed no persuasion to take it over. This is an example of the close cooperation experienced there at that time – *The Rake's Progress* had been originally planned as an Ashton ballet but de Valois eventually choreographed it.

Ballets based on other sources

We have seen how the above ballets derive for the most part from stories such as fairy tales and grand literature such as that of

Shakespeare and Cervantes. The original tale by ETA Hoffmann, *Nutcracker and the King of Mice*, which was to form Tchaikovsky's *The Nutcracker* (or *Casse Noisette*) was part of a great 19th century wave of children's stories in which the adult world looks outsize and new experiences seem overwhelming. Part of this wave were the fairy stories of Hans Christian Andersen, the early chapters of *Jane Eyre* (1847) and *David Copperfield* (1849), all of Lewis Carroll's *Alice's Adventures in Wonderland* (1865) and *Through the Looking-Glass* (1872), and Humperdinck's opera *Hansel and Gretel* (1893).

Prokofiev was commissioned to write a film score – but the film was cancelled and so he did not finish it. A copy of the partial score was found in London and has been completed by the British composer Michael Berkeley. The story is based on an episode from Dostoevsky's novel *The Idiot* and the film, *The Queen of Spades*, was to have been made in 1936. Two years later Prokofiev wrote his best known film music for Sergei Eisenstein's *Alexander Nevsky* and later for his *Ivan the Terrible*. The reworked and completed score is to be adapted for a ballet, unnamed as yet.

There are, of course, ballets based on other arts – poetry and painting. Contemporary pop music has also been used to form the basis of an ever increasing number of ballets. There are many other examples of crossing over from one genre to another – ballet derived from opera, for example. American Ballet Theatre's *Fancy Free*, which was choreographed by one of its dancer/choreographers, Jerome Robbins, was the forerunner of a musical *On The Town* which later became a film starring Frank Sinatra and Gene Kelly.

There now follows some other examples of crossovers, but before this a brief sidestep into how one must not underestimate the political effects and the use to which culture has been put, perhaps best exemplified (if a little heavy-handedly) in the charming two-act ballet *The Golden Age*, set to music by Dmitri Shostakovich. Born in 1906, this Soviet era composer and pianist, whose fame in the Soviet Union was helped by the patronage of the chief of staff, served in many government bureaucratic positions including the Supreme Soviet of the Soviet Union, from 1962 until his death in 1975. The ballet (choreography Yuri Grigorovich) is set in 1920s Soviet Russia during the period of the new economic policy, NEP, which allowed private enterprise and trade. As a result, shady operators and petty criminals are flourishing. A young dancer Rita appears under the name of Mademoiselle Margot at The Golden Age restaurant with her partner Jacques, who is in fact Yashka, a local bandit leader. They entertain a local 'fast-living, degenerate party crowd', caricatures of capitalist exploiters. Later, during the town festival, Rita meets Boris, a worker (fisherman) of an agitprop theatre. Inevitably they f… i. l..e – the reader is invited to fill in the missing letters. If you are unable to manage this, then it is regretted that these brief notes will be insufficient for your needs. Boris loses Rita, who has disappeared into the crowd. His search brings him to The Golden Age restaurant, where he recognises the dancing Mademoiselle Margot to be Rita. Boris and Yashka fight over her – she is attracted to both. Boris's fishermen friends start a brawl with the bandits, Yashka is caught but Rita escapes, leaving the restaurant forever with Boris and they l..e h….ly e..r a…r.

Alice's Adventures in Wonderland

Music: Joby Talbot Choreography: Christopher Wheeldon

Based on the well-known children's book of 1865 by Lewis Carroll, with the change that rather than being a child, Alice is a teenager beginning her first romance.

Hobson's Choice

Music: Paul Reade Choreography: David Bintley

Based on Harold Brighouse's play of the same name, this three-act ballet portrays life in a northern English town at the turn of the 19th century. It is a 'rags to riches' story, revolving around the unlikely marriage of Henry Hobson's daughter Maggie to a poor bootmaker. Talking of which, this ballet hardly deserves a sub-section to itself, but the Autumn Season 2010 of Sadler's Wells had the world premiere of *Shoes*, described as 'a dance revue that explores the gamut of footwear, from the highs of the Louboutin to the lows of the Croc'.

Ballet based on art

In 1926 Joan Miró (b. Barcelona 1893 and who, despite the name Joan, was a man) worked with Max Ernst on the set design for Sergei Diaghilev's ballet *Romeo and Juliet*.

Picasso was involved in creating the designs for nine ballets between 1917 and 1962. Two of these were created originally by Sergei Diaghilev:

***Le Tricorne (The Three-cornered Hat)* 1919**
This reflects Picasso's Spanish origins (he was a native of Andalusia) with sets, costumes and stage curtain invoking the atmosphere of a typically Spanish scene. Manuel de Falla produced the music. The story revolves around a miller's wife and her jealous husband and a senile magistrate by whom she is pursued.

***Le Train Bleu* (The Blue Train) 1924**
With the scenario being created by Jean Cocteau and costumes by Gabrielle Chanel, this is a ballet of a chic and flippant society mockingly celebrating the cult of open air life and sport. The dances are inspired by golf, tennis, swimming and acrobatics. The blue train has already left when the curtain rises and we never see it, but famed by its beautiful accessories by Lalique and marquetry by René Prou, the name evokes a certain period luxury.

Picasso also produced designs for:

1917 *Parade*
1920 *Pulcinella*
1921 *Cuadro Flamenco*
1922 *L'après-midi d'un Faune*

1924 *Mercury*
1945 *Le Rendez-vous*
1962 *Icare*

The Rake's Progress
Music: Gordon Choreography: de Valois

The theme of this ballet is the 18th century series of eight paintings from the same name by the English painter William Hogarth which achieved fame by being published in print form. They chart the decline and fall of the spendthrift son and heir of a rich merchant. They were adapted by Rex Whistler, who produced the scenery and costumes.

Miss Carter Wore Pink
Northern Ballet Theatre
Music: Joseph Horovitz Choreography: Cauley

This is a charming collection of scenes from the Edwardian childhood of Helen Bradley. Born 1900, she painted in a style not unlike that of fellow Lancastrian Lowry. She did not begin until she was over sixty, the reason being she wanted to show her granddaughter what life was like when she herself was a child. The bright pictures teem with people undertaking their normal business – an outing, funeral, market day, etc. with the same characters making an appearance: three maiden aunts, Miss Carter (who wore pink), Mr Taylor the Bank Manager, and the dogs Gyp and Barney. Her London exhibition of 1970 sold out before it opened. Shortly before her death she gave Northern Ballet Theatre two pictures, *Miss Carter's New Dress* and *Mother in Her Best Hat* with the wish that they should be sold and Northern Ballet Theatre mount a ballet based on her work.

A Simple Man

Inspired by the life and works of LS Lowry.

Music: Carl Davis Choreography: Gillian Lynne

BBC studio recording (Northern Ballet Theatre) 1987 and released on DVD by Opus Arte.

This ballet was commissioned by the BBC to celebrate Lowry's work (which is not confined to matchstick men, though this is how he is probably best known). The choreographer and the two main dancers, Christopher Gable and Moira Shearer, all come from the same background (The Royal Ballet). Gillian Lynne describes how the telling of Lowry's poignant life and the portrayal of the dogged, fatigued, resilient workforce of the British industrial scene was both exciting and intriguing and that she prefers real, earthy subjects to fantasy and fairytale. Which is probably just the opposite of the workforce! It won a BAFTA award.

Ballet 'hitching a ride on the coat tails of famous composers'

There is a particular genre of ballet where the choreographer builds on the success of famous music by building a ballet around it. This is most often contemporary greats, as in *Billboards* (Prince), *Rooster* (The Rolling Stones) etc, but Elite Syncopations capitalised on the ragtime revival made popular by the film *The Sting* and reintroduced Scott Joplin's music of the late nineteenth – early twentieth century. This is not a unique phenomenon, and hardly warrants a specific chapter as many composers have utilised current popular tunes and folk songs, most notably perhaps being Delius. It is not without its problems. In 1909 Diaghilev had made a gamble in giving Stravinsky his first large-scale commission for the Ballets Russes – this proved to be the highly successful *Firebird*. He therefore wasted no time in persuading him to use a work he had been working on in 1910 which was described as 'a sort of combat between piano and orchestra'. Material from this concert piece eventually found its place in the second tableau of the new ballet *Petrushka*.

For *Petrushka*, Stravinsky also used scraps of familiar tunes as raw material. The score abounds with Russian folk songs but there are also popular tunes such as *Elle avait une jambe de bois*. Stravinsky was sued and had to pay its publisher royalties until the 1950s (*Petrushka* received its premiere in 1911, so that was quite a time).

IRONY WARNING: in 1939 he emigrated at the age of 57 to the USA – where his ballets did not themselves enjoy any copyright protection!

Les Sylphides
Music: Chopin   Choreography: Fokine

This ballet has no story and is danced to the haunting music of Chopin, which sets the mood for the entire work. The original version was created in 1907 for a charity performance at the Mariinsky Theatre under the title *Chopiniana* – a term still retained by Russian companies. It was brought to Paris in 1909 by Diaghilev but the version usually seen now is that by Michel Fokine, produced in 1941 for the American Ballet company in New York, with Alicia Markova as ballerina.

Pineapple Poll
Music: Arthur Sullivan   Choreography: John Cranko

Most of the music comes from the Savoy operas and includes excerpts from *The Mikado, Trial by Jury, The Sorcerer, Patience, The Gondoliers, The Pirates of Penzance, Ruddigore, HMS Pinafore, Iolanthe* and *Princess Ida*. It dates from 1951 when John Cranko was looking for a typically English team on which to write a ballet for the Festival of Britain. Conveniently, Sullivan's music had just come out of copyright and it seemed natural to turn to WS Gilbert's works to find a story.

Fancy Free Ballet
Music: Leonard Bernstein   Choreography: Jerome Robbins

Three sailors find a bar where there are two girls. After a scuffle for who dances with them, each presents a solo in the nature of a competition. The girls join in the dancing but things begin to get out of hand and the girls leave.

Parade

Music: Erik Satie Choreography: Massine

This avant-garde ballet, written for the Diaghilev company and based on a theme of Jean Cocteau, was the occasion of the company's second greatest scandal (exceeded only by that caused by the *Rite of Spring*). The Cubist costumes were devised by Picasso and the form is that of a parade of three music hall acts. It begins with a Chinese conjurer, followed by an American silent film star and finally a pair of acrobats.

Enigma Variations

Music: Edward Elgar Choreography: Frederick Ashton

Ashton creates an imaginary gathering of Elgar, who is still struggling at an early stage of his career, at his Worcestershire home. Whilst waiting for a message from London, the Elgars and their friends are portrayed in various dances illustrating their personalities.

Rooster

Based on music by The Rolling Stones Choreography: David Bintley

This is one of Christopher Bruce's greatest hits and was choreographed for the Geneva Ballet. It is inspired by the hits of The *Rolling Stones* and portrays the courtship rituals of the time, together with ironic sexual warfare and quite a bit of tongue-in-cheek irony. The men are dressed in suits of the 1960s style, recreated by Bruce's wife Marian, based on Mick Jagger's original 'dandy' suit. To the music of the title tune the opening dancer struts 'rooster-like' across the stage in the courtship ritual of the time with the typical grooming gestures of slicking down the hair and adjusting the tie. Eight of the Stones' greats are represented, from the melancholy *As Tears Go By*, depicted by a couple completely ignored by three other couples, to *Lady Jane,* an affected version of a ballroom dance, to *Sympathy For The Devil* with, once again, the men and their courtship ritual.

It is available on Arthaus Musik DVD as part of a Christopher Bruce Triple Bill (with *Silence Is The End Of Our Song* and *Swansong*)

Satisfaction

Perhaps reflecting not only the popularity but also the longevity of The Rolling Stones (often referred to as the greatest rock band on earth) a second ballet has been created featuring their music. Created by the Danish choreographer Peter Schaufuss for The Schaufuss Ballet, *Satisfaction* is a Rolling Stones 'dancical'. It features 24 of the band's songs, spanning their career and including the 'greats' everybody knows. The choreography is sometimes narrative and sometimes abstract, the stage is minimal and the backdrop is by the cartoonist Gerald Scarfe. Flamboyant lighting plays around the dancers and audience, who by the end are dancing in the aisles.

Ballet For Life

Music: Queen and Mozart Choreography: Maurice Béjart.
Costumes: Versace

At the heart of this ballet is the loss to AIDS of Queen's singer, Freddie Mercury, and the dancer Jorge Donn. The collaboration of a rock band with not only the music of Mozart but also dance might initially be surprising. Queen's Roger Taylor stated: 'I would not have dared to marry our music with a ballet but what they did made me see some of our music in a different light.' Arlene Phillips is quoted: 'Freddie wanted to take ballet to the masses.' The rock influence is very apparent, with flashing lights and colours matching perfectly with Versace's costumes.

In addition to this ballet based on Queen, the Belgian choreographer Ben van Cauwenbergh was inspired by them, in particular its singer Freddie Mercury, to create a ballet in 2004 based on its many hits from the 1980s and 90s.

Billboards
Music: Prince aka The artist formerly known as Prince
Choreography: Various

This full-length rock ballet is a collaboration between a pop performer who goes under various names and The Joffrey Ballet.

Available on Warner Music Vision, 1993

Nine Sinatra Songs
Songs sung by Frank Sinatra Choreography:. Twyla Tharp

This was created by Twyla Tharp following the workings of her Sinatra-inspired duo, *Once More Frank*. She had also worked on methods of turn-of-the-century exhibition/ballroom dancing for the film *Ragtime*. Each of the Sinatra songs has its own musical and dance/theatre character, e.g. the opening, *Softly as I leave you*, is based on the theme of infatuation.

Elite Syncopations
Music: Scott Joplin Choreography: Kenneth MacMillan.

This riotous ballet with dancers dressed in outlandish colourful costumes consists of twelve self-contained short pieces danced to a collection of Scott Joplin ragtime tunes played by a small band on an otherwise bare stage. The ballet, created 1974, supported the early 1970s renaissance of ragtime music, helped by the soundtrack of the 1970's film *The Sting*.

Ballet and animals

Tales of Beatrix Potter
Music: John Lanchbery Choreography: Sir Frederick Ashton
Designer: Christine Edzard
Dancers of The Royal Ballet in association with the Royal Opera House – available on EMI video 1971

This charming ballet includes the favourite characters of Mrs Tiggy-Winkle (danced in the video by Sir Frederick Ashton), Pigling Bland, Jeremy Fisher and Squirrel Nutkin.

'Still Life' at the Penguin Café
Music: Simon Jeffes Choreography: David Bintley
The Royal Ballet – Decca Video 1991 and London Weekend TV 1987

This wonderful enchanting ballet was written by David Bintley after being inspired by records he had heard of the Penguin Café Orchestra – the creation of the musician Simon Jeffes. This comprises a small group of specialist musicians working with, as well as more conventional instruments, things as diverse as a telephone, rubber bands, etc. The ballet celebrates extinct or endangered species with the dancers dressed in animal costumes, each having its own musical piece and then joining together at the finale in a wonderful party.

Ballet based on poetry

Façade
Music: William Walton Choreography: Frederick Ashton

Towards the end of his life William Walton remarked that *Façade* had almost become his first name, so popular was this work. It was written in 1922 as an accompaniment to poems by Edith Sitwell, at whose house it was first performed that year. Ashton choreographed his first version which received its premiere in 1931 and it was quickly taken into the repertory of Marie Rambert.

Late Flowering Lust
Adventures in Motion Pictures

Based on the poetry of Sir John Betjeman, Matthew Bourne sets dances to the recitations of various poems. This was later made into a television programme set in a country house and its gardens and countryside.

Fill these pages up! JB gives a suggestion of how it might go, but be aware that anything more detailed might lead to the suspicion of an unduly organised and obsessive mind. Perhaps something along the lines of:

- **Name of ballet**
- **Venue and date**
- **Observations**

But do not be constrained! Who you were with, what you were wearing, what it all cost etc can also be added.

Ballet and celebrity

Ballet can be used by celebrities to add a touch of class to an event – as highlighted in the section Ballet and Class, ballet is seen by the advertising people as an aspirational event. Note how often ballet programmes carry adverts for high class drinks, jewellery and the like – quite different from publications such as *Women and Ammo, Monster Trucks,* etc. *The Sanguine Fan* was specially commissioned by Princess Grace of Monaco (the former actress Grace Kelly) for the International Arts Festival in Monte Carlo 1976. The only time your authors have seen pictures of Bill Clinton (the US President) in white tie was when he hosted Princess Margaret at a ballet in Washington. A rather obscure, but very commendable royal connection which the eagle-eyed will notice in the programmes of The Danish Ballet is that costume design is attributed to ... The Queen of Denmark.

So a successful ballet dancer might not only have a life in the limelight, but meet high society as well. Whilst we are about it, we should perhaps explain the phrase 'in the limelight'. Thomas Drummond invented limelight for theatres in 1816 with a machine comprising a block of lime heated to incandescence by two burning jets of gas – hydrogen and oxygen. The result was a soft, brilliant light capable of being directed and focused and also of an intensity sufficient for use in spotlights (Bennett JDC, Riddington Young J. *Offbeat Otolaryngology* Stuttgart and New York: Thieme, 2001).

A Bolshoi ballerina quit Putin's party, upset at use of her image – this was a headline to be found in *The Telegraph* on 4 February 2011. The article records how the 35-year-old prima ballerina Anastasia Volochkova said she felt she had been duped into endorsing things she did not believe in and was upset that the party had frowned upon a recent erotic photo shoot she staged at a beach in the Maldives. *The Telegraph* accompanied the reporting with a picture of her at a photo shoot in Moscow.

On the other hand, someone who has achieved celebrity status elsewhere may return to ballet. An example of this is the star usually known, because of the way she was always introduced on *Paul Daniel's Magic Show*, as 'the lovely' Debbie McGee. She trained at The Royal Ballet School and later performed with the Iranian National Ballet, her career ending early due to the political situation there. She returned to England and joined Dougie Squires' Second Generation dance troupe. She worked with the illusionist Paul Daniels in 1979 and subsequently married him. By 2000 they had set up the 'Ballet Imaginaire' (with Debbie taking the role of Choreographer and Artistic Director and Paul Daniels as Designer and Special Effects Producer) to produce touring ballet productions. Apparently, tickets sales were poor, though it is hard to see why. The first production was loosely based upon *Phantom of the Opera* with scenes from *Swan Lake* thrown in for good measure. Readers may remember a television programme made by Louis Theroux documenting the preparations. One particularly memorable part was the towing of a plywood two-dimensional swan across the stage on a rope!! Not the majestic glide they had hoped – more of a jerky lurch.

'The Arts', like many other things in life (and medicine is probably just the same) allow a step up in life into a higher social milieu. With wealth and contact with the wealthy, opportunities for travel and the finer things in life, one may be in danger of forgetting one's roots. Deborah Bull, in a short television series on dance broadcast in the nineties, took us back to her roots in Skegness (in Lincolnshire) and her humble start in dancing at a class held above a shop in the High Street. A decade later in a Radio 4 interview she was waxing lyrical about how she wanted to 'tell the man in Leeds how ballet would open his world to a hinterland which would enrich his life'. Perhaps she has never been to Leeds. Or maybe her mind was poisoned against Yorkshire by the debaters at the Oxford Union.

There definitely seems to be a certain 'pecking order' amongst ballets – and among the people who enjoy them. In this regard it is probably no different to classical music. There are those who go for the well-known 'headliners', those who have 'outgrown' these popular pieces, and those who react against them, eschewing the famous and specialising in the unknown – the more bizarre the better. One is reminded of the comments about *The Sleeping Beauty* earlier on in this chapter. The following is an actual exchange overheard during an interval:

> What is the name of this ballet (I have just heard)?
>
> The name was duly given.

They do have a very modern approach, don't they? (emphasis, in a rather derogatory tone, on modern).

Oh no, they have a proper programme as well – they do *Coppélia*!

Quite the opposite approach was taken in an article in the *Art & Entertainment Section* of the *St Louis Post-Despatch* on Sunday 22 April 2007 entitled, 'Ballet Company aims beyond 'tights and tutus''. Interesting use of the word 'beyond', I am sure you will agree. The poor journalist, who felt obliged to illustrate his full page spread with a large photograph of a dancer actually in tights and tutu, wrote in an interview style (like our introduction). His first question to the artistic director as to how he would describe his ballet company evoked the response that it was:

> 'ballet-based, but it is very contemporary. When you hear the word 'ballet' you might be expecting tights and tutus. That's not at all what we do'...'the company is very athletic, and the work that we do is very physical (!) – in the quantity of movement and in the technique of it. And the dancers are charismatic. All those qualities really set us apart and give us a unique look' (!!).

An apology must be made for the profusion of exclamation marks, but what is he talking about? Or thinking? Does he consider classical ballet not to be physical? Standing on pointe some sort of mental activity only?

In my opinion (JB) the only possible sort of justification for this sort of claptrap is to possibly increase the audience range by appealing to both contemporary and classical – i.e. come to the ballet (attracts ballet devotees) – but it is more than 'just' ballet (attracts others as well). No classical ballerina was available for comment.

There seems to be a fear that ballet might not appeal to the young as much as it should. As politicians get younger, money seems to be concentrated more amongst the young and we all aspire to seem younger than we are, then perhaps this is a worry. The reader must decide. Nevertheless, it does seem to be a concern of choreographers. Christopher Wheeldon has been described as 'the hottest kid on the block' – Debra Craine *The Times* 15 August 2007 and is alleged to be 'committed to bringing a younger audience to the art form'. Perhaps we should quote directly from his interview:

> *Winsome tutued ballerinas and fairytale productions are not the answer, he says. 'And just putting dancers in underwear on a poster doesn't make a big classical company accessible. But look at the programme that Wayne McGregor and I did in London last year. Suddenly the Royal Opera House felt vibrant and young and a lot of that was to do with Wayne's choice of music – the White Stripes. What he did, which was so successful, was to take something extremely popular and break down the boundary between popular culture and high art. I think more of that is necessary. If you can do it successfully and artistically, and in the end achieve a product that is in no way dumbing down or selling out, then you have really hit the jackpot. That's the only way to get a young audience into the theatre.'*

So there we have it. Mr Wheeldon was born in 1974. One might be reminded of the cartoon of an ageing hippy standing in front of a poster which was popular in the sixties bearing the slogan 'Never trust anybody over the age of thirty'. Thirty had been crossed out and replaced by forty, which in turn had been crossed out and replaced by fifty…

Ballet and diversity

Where are all the black swans? is a *New York Times* article written by Gia Kourlas, 6 May 2007. To quote her first paragraph directly:

> *In 1933 Lincoln Kirstein wrote a passionate letter to his friend A. Everett Austin Jr., the director of the Wadsworth Atheneum in Hartford, introducing a man named George Balanchine and a dream: to remake ballet for America. The plan, as Kerstein wrote, was to have 'four white girls and four white boys, about 16 years old, and eight of the same, negroes.'* (this was of course the language of the time)

The result of that letter, the School of American Ballet and New York City Ballet, both founded by Kirstein and Balanchine, have endured as major cultural institutions but Kirstein's plan for student diversity was never realised. Over seventy years later, the average ballet goer would be extremely surprised to find a 50:50 racial split amongst the dancers. The first, and until recently, only, black woman promoted to the rank of principal at a major American Company was Lauren Anderson of Houston Ballet – and she retired in 2006. In contrast, The Royal Ballet boasts a very eclectic mix of dancers – just read their biographies in the programme and see from what a wide range of countries they originate. This is not some new-fangled fashion. Leslie Edwards in his biography *In Good Company* describes how during the Second World War there were many dancers from many different countries. Their nationality often precluded their being called up for war service – as he was.

In order to help correct any imbalance and to widen the opportunities for dancers from ethnic minorities, some companies have been set up with the aim of catering entirely for them. Ballet Black is an up-and-coming classical ballet company with several critically acclaimed sell-out seasons to its credit. During an interview in a half-hour programme dedicated to their work (BBC 4 Sunday 23 Jan 2022) the question was posed as to why was this apparent restriction accepted when 'Ballet White' might not be? The entirely reasonable reply came that were it to be the case that white students or dancers felt under-represented and needed a 'voice', then that might be the case! Ballet Black is not only inspirational and innovative but honours the traditions of classical ballet while at the same time breaking new ground with cutting-edge choreography. In doing so, it has become a showcase for dancers of black and Asian descent. It attracts dancers, choreographers and designers from around the world. So progress is being made in tackling the idea that ballet is a bastion of white upper and middle class privilege. Nevertheless, do notice that whenever the term 'flesh coloured' is used, it always seems to assume the colour of the flesh to be a sort of pink.

Sometimes it is the actual dance piece which comes under attack, with *The Nutcracker* being accused of being 'riddled with unbelievably racist and ethnic stereotypes'. Press reports of how in The Royal Ballet's new version (*Daily Mail* 25 Jan 2022) the Arabian dance scene was altered to feature just one male and one female because of the original arrangements having 'harem' overtones. The Scottish Ballet has also fiddled with its *Nutcracker,* having amongst other things the heroine Clara's godfather Drosselmeier being played by a female, holding that:

> *To ensure it remains relevant today and for the future, we continue to make subtle, but important changes to some of the characters, costumes and choreography.*

Problems can occur when in order to satisfy one minority a different minority is harmed, which seemed to be the case when Sadler's Wells decided on cuts to their 'Company of Elders', reported in the *Daily Mail* 7 April 2019 as:

> *Furious dancers are kicked out of renowned troupe for the over-60s for being WHITE so bosses can hire more black and Asian athletes.*

Founded in 1992, this renowned dance troupe made up entirely of over-60s performers had won widespread acclaim, having performed at the National Theatre, in Japan, at the Venice Biennale, as well as being the subject of a BBC1 documentary. A spokesman for Sadler's Wells said the plan was to encourage 'people from BAME [black and minority ethnic] backgrounds… to join'. Andrew Bridgen MP pointed out that the Arts Council had given Sadler's Wells £9.8 million of public funds for the period 2018 to 2022 and that he was surprised that a publicly funded organisation would introduce such an 'ageist' policy. Trevor Phillips, the former chairman of the Equality and Human Rights Commission, commented that:

> *It's a bit scandalous to play off one minority group – people of colour – against another minority group – older dancers.'*

Ballet companies and their stages

The Royal Opera House, Covent Garden

Thanks must be recorded to Mr Barry Stewart, Director of Tours, for much of the information here.

Theatres at Covent Garden have their origin in the eighteenth century. The first was established from profits made by the aptly named actor/manager John Rich from the success of *The Beggar's Opera* (which might be considered the *Les Misérables* of the time), which he commissioned from John Gay. Newspapers had a field day with comments such as 'the arrangement made Gay rich and Rich gay'; of course, gay had a different meaning in those days!

The first building was designed by Edward Shepherd, named Theatre Royal and opened 7 December 1732. Much of Handel's work received its first London performance there, some being specially written. The organ he played was bequeathed by him with it remaining on the stage until a fire destroyed the theatre in 1808. In stark contrast to current practice, rebuilding began at once, with a foundation stone being laid on 31 December that year and the second Theatre Royal, Covent Garden opening only a few months later on 18 September 1809. It is doubtful whether that could happen nowadays. What is perhaps more surprising is that in order to finance the rebuild, seat prices had to be increased. No surprise there, you might think. But the reaction of the public was not to write a few disgruntled letters to *The Times*. Though this might well have occurred. No, direct action was the order of the day – audiences disrupted performances by beating sticks, hissing, booing and dancing. The so-called 'Old Prices' riots lasted over two months until management finally gave way. There was a wide variety of performances, with ballet and music concerts alternating with events such as Shakespeare and acrobatic performances.

The next disaster struck on 5 March 1856 with the theatre being completely destroyed again by fire. Financial considerations delayed rebuilding, but work on the third and present theatre eventually started in 1857 – a whole year later. Imagine how long it would take now! The new building was designed by Charles Barry RA (who later went on to design the Houses of Parliament) and opened the next year on 15 May 1858. The adjacent Floral Hall was built in 1860. During the day it was part of the Covent Garden fruit and vegetable market – in the evening it was a venue for dancing. In 1892 royal approval was sealed by it becoming the Royal Opera House. Winter and summer seasons of opera and ballet were given, but in between it was either closed or offered such diverse fare as film shows, cabarets, lectures or dancing.

In 1911 Diaghilev's Ballets Russes arrived, details of which are extensively recorded in other chapters. During the First World War the theatre was requisitioned by the Ministry of Works for use as a furniture repository. It was saved from this fate after the war by securing the services of Sir Thomas Beecham as artistic director in 1919. He was the heir to the giant pharmaceutical company of the same name, and used its considerable financial resources to help things along. By 1929 Diaghilev had died, leaving the House with no ballet company.

During the Second World War it became a Mecca Dance Hall. There was a possibility that it would remain a dance hall after the war but the lease was acquired by the music publishers Boosey and Hawkes, and Ninette de Valois's Sadler's Wells Ballet was invited to become the resident ballet company. There was no opera company suitable for transfer to the Royal Opera House, but a comparable resident company was started and on 14 January 1947 the Covent Garden Opera Company gave its first performance of *Carmen*. The Royal Ballet and The Royal Opera were granted their Royal Charters in 1956 and 1968 respectively.

The 'current' Royal Opera House opened on 4 December 1999. Its reconstruction actually began on site in 1996 with the last performance in the 'old' house in July 1997. It is a Grade I listed building with 2,268 seats. The orchestra pit has seven levels, being raised or lowered to suit the performance. The Royal Box has a mirror so that those sitting facing away from the stage can see the performance, but it is not liked by the Royal Family – they prefer to sit in the middle of the Grand Tier. In fact HRH Princess Margaret never used it. Or so the guides tell us. If she had never used it, how did she know she didn't like it?

But that is not all. There is also ROH2, which in the words of the programme 'is the name for the broad sweep of activity which underpins the Royal Opera House's ambition to be not just the home of two extraordinary companies, but a national resource for the nurturing and presentation of new opera, ballet, music, theatre and dance'. This is very laudable, and makes use of some of the extra space which has been found following redevelopment of the site. The rather strange, chemical formula-like name ROH2 is supported by the statement that:

> 'Behind the scenes, ROH2 provides a laboratory for the Royal Opera House…'

Readers will be relieved to know that although a 'laboratory', no white coats are needed to be worn, and no animal experimentation takes place. The gorgeous Deborah Bull is currently the creative director.

The Royal Ballet

This is the company which is based at the Royal Opera House, Covent Garden. One might have thought that this section of the book would have started with the companies, and then described their venues. This might seem more logical but, as will be seen, the 'family trees' are rather complicated, and the word 'Royal' appearing can serve to confuse. Stay with us – you are in good hands. You have just read about the story of the building in Covent Garden which came to be known as The Royal Opera House. Now let us tackle, so to speak, The Royal Ballet.

This company owes its existence to the vision of Dame Ninette de Valois, dancer, choreographer and entrepreneur, who assembled a small company and school, the Vic-Wells Ballet, so called because it performed at the Old Vic Theatre and at the Sadler's Wells Theatre in North London. In 1931 she persuaded Lilian Baylis to provide it with a home at Sadler's Wells Theatre, where they remained until 1939. September 1939 found them touring with ENSA on the Continent, returning to England in April 1940 after the fall of Holland. As the Sadler's Wells Ballet they kept going through the Blitz, but their administrative headquarters were evacuated to Burnley.

Following the cessation of hostilities a further tour was made of Germany with ENSA. Immediately afterwards, in February 1946, they transferred to the Royal Opera House, with a new full-length production of *The Sleeping Beauty* to reopen Covent Garden after its war-time suffering. Last minute rehearsals took place in partly bombed rooms in the Tottenham Court Road. De Valois continued to direct the Company through the 40s and 50s, with Frederick Ashton producing most of the new choreography. Before the war, he had already created several works that still survive today, including *Façade* (1935), *Les Patineurs* and *A Wedding Bouquet* (1937). To these were now added two acknowledged masterpieces, *Symphonic Variations*, (1946) the first new ballet to be created at Covent Garden, and *Scènes de ballet* (1948).

In 1956, to mark its 25th anniversary, the name 'The Royal Ballet' was granted by Royal Charter, and in the following year HRH Princess Margaret became President of the Company.

In 1963, Ashton succeeded de Valois as Director, continuing to create his own ballets, including *Monotones* (1965/6) and *Enigma Variations (1968).*

In 1970 Kenneth MacMillan became Director on Ashton's retirement.

In 1986 Anthony Dowell, who throughout the 60s and 70s had become the Company's leading male dancer, became Director.

In 2002 former Assistant Director of The Royal Ballet, Monica Mason was created Director following a one-year tenure by Ross Stretton, previously director of Australian Ballet.

The Royal Ballet has continued its tradition of overseas touring. Under Anthony Dowell's directorship, the company visited Australia, the Far East, Russia, Europe and the USA.

Dame Ninette de Valois maintained a close interest with The Royal Ballet and in particular The Royal Ballet School until her death on 8 March 2001, at the age of 102. Following the death of HRH The Princess Margaret in February 2002, HRH The Prince of Wales became President of The Royal Ballet in Spring 2003.

Sadler's Wells

It was in 1683 that Mr Dick Sadler opened a music house in Islington, where shortly afterwards an ancient medicinal well was found in the grounds. The name Sadler's Wells refers to the spa which soon became a (short-lived) fashionable attraction there. The summer season of entertainment filled a gap as the Theatres Royal in Covent Garden and Drury Lane operated only during autumn and winter. Eventually a new theatre was opened in 1765. Joseph Grimaldi, the great comic actor who led the development of English pantomime, was the star performer in the early years of the 19th century, introducing the pantomime dame and the tradition of audience participation. As well as pantomime, Sadler's Wells added aquatic features – in 1804 a vast tank was constructed under the stage and four years later a tank in the flies to create waterfall effects. The 19th century saw a gradual decline with conversion into a roller skating rink and later a prize fight arena. It reopened as a theatre in 1879, becoming a music hall featuring such legendary performers as Marie Lloyd. In the closing years of the 19th century it became a cinema (one of the three in London) but eventually closed in 1915.

In 1925 Lilian Baylis, who was manager of the Old Vic theatre in Waterloo, helped set up a charitable foundation designed to buy Sadler's Wells for the nation. The new theatre opened on 6 January 1931. Baylis had engaged Ninette de Valois in 1928 to present occasional ballets at the Old Vic and the first ballet performance at Sadler's Wells was on 15 May 1931 and the Vic-Wells Ballet, as it became known, became based there. Baylis had managed to create at Sadler's Wells what would become three of the top performance companies in the country: The Royal Ballet (formerly Sadler's Wells Ballet), English National Opera (formerly Sadler's Wells Opera) and Birmingham Royal Ballet (formerly Sadler's Wells Royal Ballet) as well as The Royal Ballet School.

In 1996 the company moved temporarily to the Peacock Theatre in Holborn whilst a new theatre was constructed. This opened in 1998 and also became the home of Matthew Bourne's New Adventures, Wayne McGregor's Random Dance and Christopher Wheeldon's Morphoses, an annual festival of hip hop and much more.

Birmingham Royal Ballet

In a neat link from the lines above, in addition to her role as President of The Royal Ballet, HRH Princess Margaret was also President of this company. The story is a little complicated. There are five major ballet companies in the United Kingdom: The Royal Ballet, English National Ballet, Northern Ballet and Scottish Ballet, but Birmingham Royal Ballet claims to be the UK's premier touring ballet company. It was originally founded by Dame Ninette de Valois in 1946 as Sadler's Wells Theatre Ballet, a sister company to the earlier Sadler's Wells company which moved to The Royal Opera House that year to become The Royal Ballet. It remained at Sadler's Wells as the Touring Company of The Royal Ballet, becoming Sadler's Wells Royal Ballet in 1977. Birmingham Hippodrome became its home in 1990 and in 1997 the Birmingham Royal Ballet became independent of The Royal Ballet in London, although on the website this is listed as 'sister company'. As stated at the beginning, the story is rather complicated and reminds JB of some communities he knows where Father's Day leads to similar confusion!

Ballet Rambert

Dame Marie Rambert was born Cyvia Rambam in Warsaw in 1888 and it was there that she was inspired by seeing a performance by Isadora Duncan. But in 1905, worried by her revolutionary activities, her parents advised her to go to Paris to study medicine. Using her natural talent for improvisation and composition she began to dance at fashionable houses, eventually beginning dancing school in 1910. In 1913 she was discovered by Diaghilev and invited to join his company on their South American tour. She was not re-engaged after this so in 1914 made for England to give private dancing lessons. By 1920 she was teaching ballet in her own school.

From 1926 this became known as Ballet Rambert, with an image which has always been contemporary to the times. During the war years the company reached out by performing for CEMA (Council for the Encouragement of Music and the Arts), often doing weeks of one-night stands. In doing this they were exposed to a wide audience, many of whom were seeing ballet for the first time.

In 1966 the company's policy changed completely. Dancing the classics was discontinued, with the focus being on modern dance by new choreographers, designers and composers. The idea was to get back to being a choreographers' company, making its own repertory. A new idea of allowing sculptors, designers, photographers and even ordinary visitors to watch class rehearsing and creating led to a collaboration with the Central School of Art and Design.

Diaghilev and Ballets Russes

In 1909 Serge Diaghilev began his Ballets Russes in Paris as a showcase for Russian dance in the West. By doing so he sparked a revolution that changed the face of dance in the 20th century. He developed the first real sense of bringing artists from different disciplines together and his troupe of expatriate Russians, stars such as Nijinsky and Karsavina, made dance vibrant. Bakst's lavish orientalist designs and Stravinsky's violent rhythms turned fashion and music upside down. Diaghilev was not only not a dancer, he was not even a ballet lover. He discovered his true vocation, which was to be a patron of the arts, and writing to his stepmother in 1895 he declared:

> 'I am firstly a great charlatan, though with brio; secondly, a great charmeur; thirdly I have any amount of cheek.'

From 1909 until he died in 1929 he managed to entice the most innovative and exciting names of the time: choreographers such as Fokine, Massine and Balanchine, composers such as Debussy, Ravel and Prokofiev and the painters Picasso, Braque and Matisse.

Collaborations which resulted in ballets of the Diaghilev era include:

L'après-midi d'un Faune by Nijinsky to Debussy's music.

Les Noces by Nijinska set to Stravinsky and staged by her daughter Irina.

Le Sacre du Printemps by Nijinska, also to a Stravinsky score.

In her biography Nijinska wrote of working with her brother as he developed the anti-classical postures for *Faune* and *Sacre,* which she believed signalled the birth of Modernism in dance and which she applied in her own way to *Les Noces*. In fact the premiere of *L'après-midi d'un Faune*, which had its premiere in 1912 (a year before *Le Sacre du Printemps*) had caused controversy, encouraged by the press which referred not only to the revolutionary approach to an established art form but also to the ballet's 'unabashed eroticism'. Diaghilev had made a gamble in giving Stravinsky his first large-scale commission with *The Firebird* (1909) but this proved so successful that he challenged him to produce a piece which would be a sort of 'combat between the piano and the orchestra'. This ended up as Petrushka with the first tableau having a barrel organ playing at the fair (cleverly incorporated into the score) and a prominent role for solo piano in the second.

Famous Names In Ballet And The Arts

Sir Frederick Ashton OM CH CBE 1904–1988

This most English of choreographers was in fact born in Ecuador and brought up in Peru where he saw Pavlova dance. Family pressure pushed him to an English public school and a job in the city where he secretly began to take ballet lessons. By good fortune, he started with Massine who recommended that he continue his studies with Marie Rambert. There were no permanent British ballet companies in those days but she arranged engagements for her pupils and also encouraged him to try choreography. Whilst spending a year as a dancer in Ida Rubinstein's company Ashton had the chance to work under Bronislava Nijinska (sister of Vaslav Nijinsky), teaching himself a lot about choreography by watching the way she worked. Back in Britain he helped to found the Ballet Club which later became Ballet Rambert and in 1931 created his first work for Ninette de Valois' young company. He remained as her associate while the company grew to become The Royal Ballet, succeeding her as director in 1963. He held this position for seven years before officially retiring in 1970. More details of his work for the company can be found in the section 'The Royal Ballet'.

Pina Bausch 1942–2009
Dancer and choreographer, company founder Tanztheater in Wuppertal, Germany

Sir Matthew Bourne OBE b 1960
He started training to be a dancer at the comparatively late age of 22, studying dance theatre and choreography at the Laban Centre then spending a further year with the college's performing company. He danced professionally for 14 years, giving his final performance in 1999, but during 1987 to 2000 was also artistic director of his first company, *Adventures in Motion Pictures.* This became the United Kingdom's most innovative and popular dance theatre company, winning awards too numerous to mention. In 2002 he launched, along with co-director Robert Noble, the company *New Company.* The new production of *Nutcracker*! received its premiere at Sadler's Wells in 2002 and was the first ballet to be screened by BBC 1 in over 20 years. Following a world tour his production of *Swan Lake* continues to tour and the dance-thriller *The Car Man* has achieved widespread recognition outside of traditional ballet audiences.

Leo Delibes 1836–1891
Delibes was trained at the Paris Conservatoire with his first major triumph being the ballet *Coppélia,* based on a story by Hoffmann and staged in 1870. He followed this in 1876 with *Sylvia,* set in pagan Greece.

Dame Ninette de Valois 1898–2001
Founder of The Royal Ballet Companies and The Royal Ballet School, she was born in Ireland and started dancing under several teachers there. She made her professional debut as a principal dancer in 1914 in pantomime at the Lyceum Theatre and by 1919 had become principal dancer with the Beecham Opera at Covent Garden. During 1922 she danced with Massine's and Lopokova's companies at Covent Garden and the Coliseum, joining the Diaghilev ballet in 1923 and rising to the rank of

soloist. By 1926 she had left the company to found her own school of dancing – the first step in achieving her ambition of founding a British ballet company. In order to give her pupils professional experience she offered them to Lilian Baylis, director of the Old Vic Theatre to appear in opera and Shakespearean productions there. In 1931 Lilian reopened the Sadler's Wells Theatre and de Valois moved her school there, engaging Frederick Ashton as guest choreographer in 1933.

Sir Anthony Dowell CBE b 1943

Director of The Royal Ballet 1986–2001, was created Knight Bachelor in 1995 for services to ballet. Throughout the 60s and 70s he was The Royal Ballet's leading male dancer. He produced new versions of the two most famous classical ballets in the repertory for the company: *Swan Lake* (1987) and *The Sleeping Beauty* (1994). Both remain faithful to the original Petipa choreography as it was handed down to de Valois' young company. He also capitalised on the new talent which had emerged and developed under his eye, notably Darcey Bussell, Alina Cojocaru, Viviana Durante and Sarah Wildor,

Dame Margot Fonteyn 1919–1991

Born as Peggy Hookham, she felt that her chances would be better as Margot Fonteyn. She attended her first ballet class in Ealing just before the age of five and by eighteen was seen dancing on the new BBC television service (but not by many, as only a few hundred owned sets). At the age of 42, when it might have been considered that her career was approaching its end, she danced with Rudolf Nureyev to such acclaim that it rejuvenated her career, with him becoming her principal partner in The Royal Ballet.

La Goulue 1866–1929

Also known as Queen of Montmartre, she was born Louise Weber but got her nickname ('goulu' means greedy in French) from her habit of drinking from customers' glasses. She achieved fame as a cancan dancer at the Parisian dance hall Le Moulin Rouge, but is more known by appearing in a promotional poster, which made the name of the artist Henri de Toulouse-Lautrec.

Martha Graham 1894–1991

In its 26 May 2021 edition *Time* magazine named her 'dancer of the century' and *People Magazine* named her among the 'icons of the century'. When you consider the biographies of some of the other names in this section, that is either incredibly high praise, or a rather insular nationalistic view taken by these magazines. The reader must decide. She has been described as an influential American dancer, teacher, and choreographer of modern dance whose ballets and other works were intended to 'reveal the inner man.' Feminists may baulk at the word 'man', but it is a direct quote from Encyclopaedia Britannica. It is considered that 'she gave new depth as a vehicle for the intense and forceful expression of primal emotions', doing this in the 180-plus works she created over 50 years.

Sylvie Guillem CBE b 1965

Danced with Paris Opera Ballet 1984–1989 then principal guest artist with The Royal Ballet. She also performed contemporary dance with Sadler's Wells, finally retiring from dance, but not the dancing world, at the age of 50.

Robert Joffrey 1930–1988

Founder of the company (1956) which bears his name, Joffrey was a gifted choreographer, renowned dance teacher and inspired director, presenting wonderful reconstructions and revivals of 20th century classics. Perhaps the most significant was his company dance, Vaslav Nijinsky's lost ballet, *Le Sacre du Printemps,* which had not been performed since its premiere in 1913. It was commonly believed that only a few sketches and memoirs remained of this original but in 1971 a graduate student, Millicent Hodson, showed interest in the project and, encouraged by Joffrey, began the painstaking process of recording every detail known. This was principally through annotated scores belonging to

Stravinsky and Rambert but also through artist sketches, memoirs etc involving research and interviews throughout the world.

Kenneth MacMillan 1929–1992

He started his choreographic career with The Royal Ballet's 'sister' company, Sadler's Wells Theatre Ballet, (which had been created to dance at Sadler's Wells Theatre after the original Company's departure to the Opera House) before making works for the Covent Garden stage. He became Director on Ashton's retirement in 1970. Both choreographers continued to create for the Company, with Ashton producing another acknowledged masterwork, *A Month in the Country* (1976), followed by *Rhapsody* (1980), and MacMillan contributing full-length ballets including *Manon* (1974) and *Mayerling* (1978) and one-act works ranging from the jazzy *Elite Syncopations* (1974) to the elegiac *Gloria* (1980). He choreographed *The Prince of the Pagodas* in 1989 to show, for the first time, the talents of the young Darcey Bussell, then aged nineteen, and created works for the Company up until his death in 1992, aged sixty-two.

Alicia Markova 1910–2004

Born with the name Lily Marks, she changed it whilst training in Russia. She performed with the Ballets Russes and the English National Ballet and was probably the first internationally recognised British ballet dancer, appearing on British television in a production of *Les Sylphides* in 1953.

Dame Monica Mason DBE b 1941

Coming from South Africa to England at the age of 14 to train at The Royal Ballet School, she joined the company when she was only 16 (the youngest member at that time). Following a brief period in the Corps she was selected by Kenneth MacMillan for *The Rite of Spring* and a year later, in 1963, was appointed soloist, finally becoming a principal in 1968. 1984 saw her appointment as Principal Répétiteur to The Royal Ballet and in 1991 she became Assistant Director followed by Director and the award of an OBE in 2002 after the resignation of Ross Stretton. She was created a Dame Commander in 2008 for her services to dance and was Director until 2012.

Bronislava Nijinska 1898–1972
The sister of Vaslav Nijinsky, born in Minsk to Polish ballet dancer parents (hence the female ending to her surname). She began at the Vaganova Academy in St Petersburg (yes, you read about this in the ballet classes in the 'Childhood' section), graduated to the Russian Imperial Ballet, which she left in 1911 as a protest against her brother's dismissal. She danced with Ballets Russes in Paris, returning to Russia during the First World War and Revolution, then leaving for good in 1921. She was also an innovative choreographer. She moved to California in 1938, thereby presumably justifying being called an American dancer and choreographer in some biographies.

Vaslav Nijinsky 1890–1950
Studied from 1898 at the Vaganova Academy, he graduated in 1907 and joined the Mariinsky Theatre as a soloist that same year. In 1909 Sergey Diaghilev, former assistant to the administrator of the Imperial Theatres, was commissioned to organise a ballet company of the members of the Mariinsky and Bolshoi theatres. He decided to take the company to Paris in the spring and asked Nijinsky to join as principal dancer. He created for Diaghilev's Ballets Russes the ballets *L'Après-midi d'un faune, Jeux,* and *Le Sacre du Printemps.* The reader of a book written primarily by a doctor would rightly feel disappointed were there not to be some medical nuggets. As has been covered elsewhere, performances can be delayed and there are many occasions when the topic of conversation needs to be steered away from contentious issues. Furthermore, medical issues are often almost favourite obsessions, as doctors at dinner parties find to their cost. Anyway, in early 1919, at the age of 29 and overwhelmed by turmoil about the end of his career, devastation at the recent war and mental stress from which he had suffered throughout his life, Nijinsky became consumed by psychosis. He documented this in a diary written over a frantic six weeks,

beginning writing the evening of his final performance (which saw him facing his audience for 30 minutes seated on a chair). His writing describes a complex delusional system with the suggestion of auditory hallucinations. His wife Romola took him to see the local doctor and tried to conceal medication in his food. He was then sent to see Eugen Bleuler (the notable Swiss psychiatrist who coined the term schizophrenia) where he received insulin therapy and other early treatments, but went on to spend most of his life in psychiatric institutions, finally dying in London in 1950 but being buried in the cemetery of Montmartre in Paris.

Anna Pavlova 1881–1931

Like so many others stars, she started at the Vaganova Academy from 1891, joining the Imperial Ballet in 1899. She became a prima ballerina in 1906 and became associated with the revolutionary ideas of Michael Fokine, who choreographed the famous *Dying Swan* for her. 1909 saw her dancing with Diaghilev's Ballets Russes in Paris, featuring on the poster advertising the season. In 1912 she bought a house in north London which became her permanent home. It had a huge garden with a large pond with swans, which she studied to bring realism to her most famous role, *The Dying Swan*. In 1913 she resigned from the Russian Imperial Ballet and formed her own company. Worn out by touring and the stress of performing she died of pneumonia in 1931, aged just 51. It was in 1926 on a tour of Australia and New Zealand that the dessert pavlova (a crisp meringue shell topped with whipped cream and fruit) was developed – each country claiming credit. Apparently a meringue is crispy and dry throughout, while pavlova is crispy on the outside, but fluffy, soft and marshmallow-like on the inside.

Marius Petipa 1818–1910

Born in France, he went to St Petersburg in 1847 as principal dancer of the Imperial Ballet. His debut as a choreographer came in 1849 and 20 years later he took entire charge of the Mariinsky Company, producing for them his greatest works: *La Bayadère* (1877) *Sleeping Beauty* (1890), *Swan Lake* (1895) and *Raymonda* (1898).

Sergei Prokofiev 1895–1953

Russian composer, pianist and conductor who graduated from the St Petersburg Conservatory but broke away from the standard composer-pianist role with an orchestral suite compiled from music originally composed for a ballet commissioned by Diaghilev. He also commissioned three further ballets from him: *Chout, Le Pas d'Acier* and *The Prodigal Son*. Following the Revolution in 1917 he left for the USA and is perhaps best known for his opera *The Love for Three Oranges* (composed for the Chicago Opera). Following his return to the Soviet Union in 1934 after many years in the West his mood musical compositions were influenced by the prevailing traditions and culture-political climate in Moscow. Soviet audiences wanted single-feature ballets with an intense dramatic content and beautiful, easily understood music closely bound to the great classical traditions. Hence his *Romeo and Juliet* (composed 1935) continues the grand symphonic dramatic ballet tradition as established by Tchaikovsky.

Galina Stepanenko b 1966

Born in Moscow, from 1984-88 she was a soloist with the Moscow Classical Ballet, then the Moscow Academic Company (yes, they have a lot of ballet companies there) before being invited to join the Bolshoi Ballet in 1990, becoming a prima ballerina. Since 2013 she has been head of the Bolshoi Ballet troupe. In 1992 she completed her studies at the Russian Academy of Theatre Art, qualifying as a teacher choreographer.

Arthur Michel St-Léon 1821–1870

Somewhat overshadowed by his contemporary and fellow countryman Marius Petipa, the multi-talented St-Léon played a major part in the musical theatre of the 19th century. He was a dancer, choreographer, violinist, composer and the inventor of a system of dance notation. He produced his first ballet in London while still only 23, made his debut in St Petersburg at the age of 38, becoming Maître de Ballet of the St Petersburg Imperial Ballet 1859-1869, then later at the Paris Opéra where he produced a string of successful ballets, the last being his masterpiece *Coppélia*.

A short history of fashion and the arts

(inc. some technological developments!)

We first begin with a cautionary tale and how a little knowledge, particularly when used to overanalyse things, can be detrimental. This is especially so in social situations as the following example will demonstrate. To set the scene, we must first explain that for many years JB has benefitted from the friendship of a German ENT surgeon specialising not only in voice but also many other aspects of Arts as applied to medicine. She has written widely about medical conditions seen in paintings and whenever we visit a gallery together, the trip takes far longer, but is far more informative and enjoyable. Anyway, we were at a colleague's house, and whilst awaiting his return, his wife proudly showed us into the drawing room (not a room set aside for drawing and sketching but an old-fashioned term for where one 'withdraws' after leaving the dining room). Above the mantelpiece hung a reproduction painting, which had probably been a wedding present. The wife was intensely proud of it, drawing it to our attention and remarking how homely it was – it was a picture of a bedroom. But Dr Brosch (now Professor, despite this faux pas) knew better. It showed the misery and despair of the painter and was highly symbolic. The twin pillows on the single bed drew attention to the lover he had lost, the untidiness of his chaotic life, etc. She pointed out that not long after completing this work, the artist had committed suicide. I thought the wife was going to cry. It was no longer hanging there on my next visit.

Anyway, despite all this, it is generally thought useful to have an overview of what was going on in a wider sense so that ballet can be put into some sort of context. But let us be sensible about this – remember, a good scientific theory should be explicable to a barmaid. So it is with the Arts – do not to fall into the trap of overanalysing. But when one understands what changes were occurring at the time in terms of costume and fashion, music, etc. then one can appreciate the dance even more. But be careful!

Dance is an age-old phenomenon and one of the most basic human actions. Play some music and someone will dance. For many years the history of ballet and ballroom were the same, practised only by the aristocracy. But in the late 17th century, the notion of the performing professional dancer was introduced and dancing moved out of the court and onto the stage. Another milestone was the early 19th century when dancing became somewhat risqué and the modern waltz hold was introduced. Before this, dancers were separated by a physical space. When the new hold arrived it was forbidden in some gatherings, with young debutantes being persuaded that it was not proper! However, by the start of the 20th century women were dancing with a new equality instead of being led around the dance floor. The tango became fashionable for a while (introduced to London from Paris in 1911) with tango parties but this proved to be a short-lived fad. Jazz, with its improvisation and free rhythms superseding ragtime (both from America) brought about a musical revolution. New dances were born from the jazz age such as tap dancing, the cakewalk, the two-step, the bunny hug and, most famous of all, the Charleston. Perhaps the most famous dancer of this era is Josephine Baker (1906 – 1975), an American born erotic dancer who found fame in Paris with her 'banana dance'.

De Lafontaine 1655–1738 considered to be the first professional female dancer Paris Opera.

1820 To facilitate shopping, the covered bazaar was introduced in Paris.

1840 Safety pin invented by Walter Hunt.

1844 The chemist Mercer invents Silkaline from cotton.

1846 Elias Home invents a machine for sewing leather shoes.

1850 Blue jeans invented by Levi Strauss.

1855 George Audemars patents viscose – the world's first artificial fibre.

The first fashion houses began to appear mid-19th century with labels with the name of the designer – such as Charles F Worth. A woman's silhouette at this time was characterised by the fullness of her skirt, something achieved by layers of petticoats or the metal framework of the hoop skirt. The final third of the nineteenth century led to developments in transport which made the crinoline impractical and led to the much smaller bustle of the Romantic period being adopted. This was formed by a cushioned shape, starched flounces and whalebone or metal hoops sewn onto the underskirt which supported metres of material gathered over the hips. The resulting posture, along with such a prominent posterior, invited a comparison with poultry. Note how in the ballet *Rooster*, the men's jackets are cut with a high flared waist to give a similar effect. Women's silhouettes changed radically as the more vertical line became fashionable and portraits show an outline very different from earlier times. The parasol became an indispensable part of female attire and was carefully chosen to match the hat and dress. As with the fan, a conventional coded language was developed by which meanings were attributed to its position and movements, but this will be left to more specialised books!

1868 Chemical dyes patented by Henry Perkin.

1875 New Paris opera house opened, Palais Garnier, named after its architect Charles Garnier. His building must be seen by the reader rather than any written description here, save for the fact that he designed a mirrored foyer for backstage, writing, 'as a setting for the charming swarms of ballerinas, in their picturesque and coquettish costumes.'

1885 Metal snaps introduced – initially on gloves.

1889 Eiffel Tower completed, taking two years, two months and five days of work.

1892 Vogue founded in New York (taken over by the publisher Condé Nast in 1909).

1893 Zipper invented by Whitcomb Judson.

1894 London Tower Bridge was built – a masterpiece of hydraulics.

1898 First public escalator – in a store in London's Crystal Palace. That same year Harrods followed suit with the refinement that brandy was provided for nervous men (women were offered smelling salts).

The end of the 19th century saw the first appearance of the bra, which was in effect a corset cutaway below the breast. It was not, however, until 1961 that the so-called Wonderbra appeared, made by Louise Poirier in Canada. Over a hundred years after its introduction, it is reported that the majority of women are still not wearing a correctly fitting bra. Also reported is the research that most women refer to a front-fastening bra, whilst men call it a front-opener. The subjects universities devote resources to never fail to amaze. Surveys have shown that the Scots are the happiest people in the world. Which just goes to show that university researchers do not understand sarcasm!

The wearing of black for mourning began in the Romantic period, generally thought to be at its peak 1800-1850. Jet was considered the most appropriate material for mourning jewellery and it was not long before less expensive imitations were being developed. French jet was a blend of black glass and lead which could be moulded. Ebonite (Goodyear 1844) was produced by the vulcanisation of rubber with sulphur and could be worked on a lathe. Nowadays black seems to be worn to everything. In fact JB was once reliably informed by a young German woman at the Goethe Institut in Berlin, where he was studying, that black matches everything. She wasn't just talking about shirts. If we are going to talk about fashion it might be appropriate at this point to re-emphasise that when you are good-looking, it doesn't matter what you wear. Or if you have many other things on your mind. It is recorded that Marie Curie was married in a dark blue dress, which she then wore to work in her laboratories until it wore out. That is the way to get two Nobel prizes!

Edgar Degas 1834–1917

Born in Paris, his specialty was the ballet dancer – reproduced not only in pencil and chalk drawings, monotype prints and pastels, oil paintings, but also sculptures – the most celebrated being *Little Dancer, Aged Fourteen*. His painting, *La classe de danse*, shows all the dancers with a black ribbon around the neck, for reasons which are not quite clear.

Auguste Rodin 1840–1917

At the age of fourteen, young Auguste enrolled at the École Impériale de Dessin, commonly known as the 'Petite École' to distinguish it from the École des Beaux-Arts. He learnt there the importance of natural light to enhance forms, leading him to state later that 'sculpture is an art of the open air'. He was refused three times at the École des Beaux-Arts and so began work as an ornamentalist in the studio of Carrier-Belleuse. By the dawn of the twentieth century he had become an undisputed master.

Impressionism

The paintings of those who were later to be known as 'Impressionists' were all rejected by the jury of the salon of 1867 (Paris). This was nothing new – when Courbet's work was not accepted at the International Exhibition of 1855 he had the Pavilion of Realism built at his own expense to show Parisians his work. The salon des refusés organised in 1863 is another example. There are many such examples even to this day – the Beatles and J K Rowling all had doubters who felt there was no future for guitar bands and Harry Potter. The first showing organised by Pissaro, Renoir, Monet and Degas took place in 1874 in a studio offered by the photographer Nadar, with a painting by Monet: *Impression, Sunrise* creating a stir. The former refusés were censured as being 'Impressionists' – a name they would later willingly assume.

Neo-impressionism

The Eighth Impressionist Exhibition, 1886, assembled some of the Impressionist painters for the last time, but also introduced two young painters: Georges Seurat and Paul Signac. Seurat's *Sunday Afternoon on the Island of Grande-Jatte* caused a scandal (the French do seem to have been easily scandalised in those days!) with its new technique of divided brush strokes. He called his method 'chromoluminarisme' and it had the stated aim of making art an exact science by adopting two scientific principles.

First, from the law of simultaneous contrasts formulated by the chemist Chevreul, whereby a colour appears to be surrounded by a faint aureole of its complementary colour. Thus a green tinted sky will be seen around a red roof.

Second, the principal of optical mixture – two juxtaposed colours produce more intensity than would be achieved by mixing.

His technique therefore was to break up the tones into a pattern of tiny dots of pure colour which are then fused by the viewer's eye. To increase the luminosity of the colour even more, they were applied evenly on a white background – he even preferred white frames.

Symbolism

This emerged during the last decades of the 19th century, beginning primarily as a literary movement for poetry with the visual arts following. There was a taste for myths and dreams and of idealised female forms in a so-called Golden Age.

1896 Khaki uniforms were introduced into the British Army – it was found that the white uniforms worn in the Sudan were much less conspicuous after they had become stained with dust and mud.

Belle Epoque 1898–1914

1899 The Royal Opera House was wired for electric lighting, replacing gas which could never be completely turned off, only turned down. Consequently up to this point the House had never been in complete darkness.

Naturalism (this is nothing to do with nudists – that is naturism) This term initially applied to a philosophical movement which considered nature as being the origin of everything – thus rejecting the notion of God. In the domain of the fine arts from the 17th century on, 'Naturalists' were artists who considered it necessary to faithfully imitate nature. A 'Naturalist School' emerged by the second half of the nineteenth century, headed by the writer Emile Zola. Between 1871 and 1893 he published twenty novels concerning a 'family's natural and social story during the Second Empire' – that is the French empire. In painting, Naturalism extended the precepts of realism, adopting 'modern subjects' such as agricultural life, industrial labour and things which had previously been considered unworthy. The movement spread rapidly from France throughout Europe and by the turn of the century was one of the strongest official movements. The Symbolist Movement, which developed simultaneously, denounced it for its lack of idealism and spirituality.

1906 Paul Poiret abandons the corset in ladies' clothing

1907 Braque and Picasso launch the Cubist movement. This was developed in Montmartre by the Spanish émigré Pablo Picasso and the French artist Braque. It is an abstract style of art which attempts to represent the view of an object from all viewpoints at once. Never agree to be operated on by any cosmetic surgeon who professes to love Cubist art! The story is told of how Picasso's house was burgled. Picasso very helpfully drew a picture of the robber and the police subsequently arrested a horse and two sardines.

1910 Ballets Russes premier of *The Firebird*.
Stravinsky was twenty-eight at the time. He had temporarily set aside ballet composition and began work on a concert piece which he called 'a kind of combat between piano and orchestra'. It had the starting point, musically, of the clash of two major triads, on C and F sharp – or 'white notes versus black'. By September 1910, when Diaghilev and Nijinsky visited him, the piece had developed a story (about a puppet

with human feelings) and the title *Petrushka*. Diaghilev saw possibilities beyond the concert platform and it was completed that winter as a four-scene ballet. It received its premiere by the Diaghilev ballet at the Théâtre du Châtelet, Paris on 13 June 1911 and was presented at Covent Garden in 1912.

1910 Coco Chanel opens her first Paris shop. The outdoor life and sport began to influence what was worn. In this decade Coco Chanel popularised the sun tan after returning to Paris from a holiday in the French Riviera. Prior to this it had been considered rather vulgar and a sign of manual outdoor labour. Now it reflected the emancipated outdoor woman.

1911 First escalator on the London Underground (Earl's Court).

1912 Elastic girdles introduced

1912 Paris premiere of Nijinsky's *Faune* with its explicitly erotic fantasy causing a scandal. This was the only Nijinsky ballet to be notated, with he himself writing it down in his own idiosyncratic hand. None of the performances were filmed and so choreography of revival ballets is difficult. It must be remembered that ballet tends to be an ephemeral art (apart from video recordings). It is comparatively easy to lay down laws and precepts concerning musicians and painters, we can also refer back to them. In contrast, when a dancer has danced, the only thing which remains of the performance is the length of time it will live in the minds of those who saw it. Fortunately, the music survives and is still played. Pictures abound of the magnificent sets and costumes, with many of the originals being held in museums around the world.

1913 *The Rite of Spring*
The First World War introduced a more practical look, with emancipation of women following in its wake.

1914 Burberry manufactures Trench/21 coat for soldiers

1918 British women get the vote (so long as they are over 30 and meet a property qualification).

1919 Sex Disqualification Removal Act in Britain – this changed the law which barred women's entry to the professions. Women could now stand for Parliament, become vets, architects, civil servants, lawyers, sit on juries.

1919 Bauhaus (building house) School founded by Walter Gropius with the idea of embracing machine culture so that construction of buildings, furniture etc could be utilitarian yet beautiful in that they were effective and functional. The belief is that the artist and the craftsman act as one. This does not always work out as intended – as witnessed by the Millennium foot bridge across the Thames which sways when the wind blows. David Hockney's design for a telephone book for the city of Bradford was so good that everybody stole them. A similar thing happened to posters advertising Stephen Fry's play *Latin* at the Edinburgh Festival so that he had to resort to defacing them slightly so that they would become less attractive to thieves.

1920 First French edition of *Vogue*

1928 Nylon invented but mass production would be delayed until 1938.

We have seen how corsets and girdles were used to compress (hoop skirts and bustles had done the opposite). In the 1920s women wore dresses 'à la garcon', with straight lines and no waist. Fashion was becoming closely linked to the Art Deco craze and the emerging avant-garde in art: Orphism, Cubism, Surrealism. Painters like Dalí, Picasso, De Chirico, Matisse and Sonia Delaunay involved themselves in the world of fashion, designing fabrics and stage costumes.

There was functionalism in all arts – dresses were short with straight, clean lines. Shoulder straps were thin and adorned with fringes that moved to the rhythm of the Charleston. The tango dress was larger, draped and with a low back which gave more freedom of movement.

Art Deco aimed at glamour, though it might come as a surprise to learn that much of the London Underground (railway rather than subversive movement) style was originally Art Deco. This was especially for the advertisements which wanted to show a more glamorous life than that probably experienced by the average commuter. Some movements, such as Modernism, Arts and Crafts, exuded a form of moral earnestness, exhorting us to lead the sort of life they extolled. This was not the case with Art Deco – this was about glamour, and not just glamour but sexual allure to boot. In the 1920s, even machinery became eroticised – look at objects such as trains, boats, and even household objects. Much of the London Underground style was originally Art Deco, in particular the advertisements. There was an almost touching belief that after the horror of world war, material things gave glamour to those who owned them. This is something that has perhaps been replicated recently by 'designer-labelled' objects. The trend was linked firmly with female emancipation. Clothes and settings were established that made women look good. Look at their clothes, film sets, furniture. It concentrates on simple abstract forms and straight lines (in contrast to the swirling forms of nature found in Art Nouveau, as can be seen in many of the Paris Metro original station frontages designed in the Art Nouveau style and which remain intact to this day) with an emphasis on smooth surface decorations. It flourished in the economic boom of the 1920s and became the international style for the luxury market. An important woman figure in the world of art at this time was the Polish woman painter, Tamara de Lempicka, with her voluptuous 'pin-up' like women in fast cars.

Dancers were also not to be found lacking. It was during the Art Deco period in 1925 that the American entertainer Josephine Baker and her act, *La Revue Nègre*, took Paris by storm with her 'danse sauvage'. She performed this almost nude, turning her whole body into a zig-zagging Art Deco pattern. Her hair was brilliantined down onto her head so that it looked like lacquer. The show opened at the Théatre des Champs-Élysées. This is not on the Avenue des Champs-Élysées but near the Place de l'Alma end of Avenue Montaigne (which has all the posh dress shops) where it forms an equilateral triangle with the end of Avenue George V (which has The Crazy Horse Club). Readers who know all this will just have to be patient – others might not.

Fashion Renewal 1939–1959

1935 First 'shorts' appear in Hollywood.

1941 Terylene, the first polyester fibre, developed by John Rex Whinfield.

1945 Nylon stockings marketed around the world by Dupont.

1946 Bikinis presented in Louis Réard's swimwear collection.

1948 *Constance* came out in March as one of the first new post-war women's magazine. In the 1950s it became one of the most popular magazines in Germany with a print run of 575,000.

1948 Velcro was invented by George de Mestral.

1950s cinema began to have ever more influence on fashion. The knitjacket 'Rebecca' became popular after the film of that name and Casablanca set off a craze for trench coats. Audrey Hepburn popularised Dior's *New Look* with her narrow and sloping shoulders and flowing skirts. Dior had been catapulted to fame in 1947 with his very first collection – suits with rounded shoulders, short tailored jackets over simple skirts, wasp waists and full skirts cut at the knee. He actually called it the *Corolle*, but US journalists called it *The New Look* – and that is what stuck. A great novelty was the cocktail dress – more elegant than the afternoon dress but less formal than the evening dress.

1957 BBC transmits a new programme, *6-5 Special*, which was aimed at teenage dancers.

1959 *Sleeping Beauty* was broadcast live by the BBC.

1960 Transistor radio.

1961 The first 'wonderbra' made by Canadian Louise Poirier.

1962 BBC develops a programme entitled *Twist* (after the popular dance).

1963 Philip Larkin considered this to have been the year that sex became more widely talked about and describes this in a poem. Let Google be your friend!

1963 American Express credit card launched in UK. It is hard to imagine how one would order and pay for ballet and opera tickets without credit cards nowadays.

1977 *Saturday Night Fever* popularised disco dancing and heralded the return of people going to a dance studio to learn disco moves. Fitness videos, popularised by Jane Fonda, closely followed and were replicated by, it seemed, every actress and TV personality.

1980 *Fam*e – a television series set in a school of music and dance first aired in Britain.

1981 Russell Harty introduced on his television show the dance group *Hot Gossip*, the brainchild of Arlene Phillips. Her claim was that they had no money for costumes, drawing on gifts of clothes from a friend's sex shop. In her words, the scanty revealing outfits 'allowed free movement of the body'. No doubt they also increased the viewing figures.

1984 The BBC transmitted a documentary about acrobatic break dancing from New York.

1996 The BBC aired a 'behind the scenes' look at The Royal Ballet in a documentary, *The House*. Naturally, emphasis was placed on arguments between staff about funding and the difficulties Darcy Bussell was having in rehearsing *The Sleeping Beauty* premier in front of the US President.

1998 *Come Dancing* was taken off air.

1998 Darcy Bussell appeared in a spoof of ballet with Dawn French in her television series *The Vicar of Dibley,* thus popularising and bringing ballet to a more general public.

2004 *Strictly Come Dancing* first televised. This is based on competitive ballroom dancing but, unlike *Come Dancing,* used celebrities – the dancers were not necessarily good, but got better during the course of the competition. There is also a typical pantomime villain / clown, and kitsch became chic. It has reached audiences up to 10 million and its success has been repeated around the world.

INTERMISSION

Well, it is amazing how time flies and here we are in the middle of the book. A lot of the 'big stuff' has been covered and it is all downhill from now on. So take a break. Our research has shown that most readers have been reading just about non-stop up to this point! So relax, wind down and just think over what a good purchase you have made in this book. Why, the purchase price barely covers a couple of skinny decaff double latte hold-the-chocolate blah, blah, blah and a muffin (what used to be called a bun, which was about half the size and a fifth the price).

Lie back and relax.

The rest is really good, and very easy.

No, this is not a con – and not at all like what has become to be known as 'The Ceramic Hob Incident'.

A very dear friend (pun is intended) threw her ashtray in a fit of pique, and it landed on the ceramic hob, breaking it. This information was relayed by telephone to JB at three in the morning. But was JB downhearted? Of course not. Magazines, advice columns, housewife gossip, etc. are full of minor mishaps such as this, and so despite the early hour, these sources of help were suggested, together with something along the lines of:

The answer probably lies in wiping the surface with a soft cloth moistened with vinegar, then applying nail varnish to the crack.

Or, at worst: Apply cling film, then lightly press with a steam iron.

You know the sort of thing.

How wrong can you be?

What a con. The final solution was a new oven, costing 570 euros. Euros? This was in Berlin, which somewhat puts paid to the myth that the Prussian is efficient, careful, methodical, etc. Anyway, I was glad to pay it – she is a dear friend. But what a con. There must be mountains of perfectly good cookers in working order lying somewhere just waiting for new ceramic hobs.

Rest assured, there are no nasty shocks like that in the rest of this book. Short paragraphs, a bit of scandal and gossip. Some racy bits for the dads and lads. We know what you want. You are in safe hands.

But while we are on about cons, please allow JB the indulgence of another rant, particularly as this intermission is taking place in the privacy and comfort of your own home, or wherever you are choosing to read this.

Unless you happen to be in the Royal Opera House, you are not being put in the position of having to fork out £4, yes, FOUR POUNDS for an ice cream. Well, that is not too bad, you may be thinking. At Quaglionoronio's a kiwi and passion fruit sherbet amuse bouche costs far more. Yes, but that is where bloated businessmen take their secretaries as a special reward for working late and clinching that big contract (or so we are told!). But we are talking about a tiny plastic tub with a tiny plastic spatula which can only in its dreams aspire to being called a spoon. Why so small? Well, the stated contents of the tub are only 120 ml. If you were given a proper spoon then that would be just over a couple of mouthfuls. There must be a better way of making money than from children like this. The reader is advised to reread the chapter 'The Stage and Working Conditions' about cheap and expensive seats. Anyway, enough of the rant.

We now need to move onto another feature found in this book, but sadly lacking in lesser volumes, where its requirement is often far more pressing. It is the aim of a book such as this to reveal THE INTERESTING THINGS and be INTERACTIVE and allow the reader a COMPREHENSIVE LEARNING EXPERIENCE etc. etc. Unfortunately the one thing that cannot be replicated in these pages, and which the organisers of conferences are so fond of, is inviting participants (or, as they are rather bizarrely known now, 'attendees') to BREAK OUT INTO SMALL GROUPS.

But your writing team is nothing if not resourceful and suggests you step down from the lectern, arise from your desk, armchair or whatever circumstances you find yourself in to read this book. Seek out a family member or pet. Regale them with the success of your purchase and your new-found knowledge. Suffer their envy with quiet fortitude. Bask in their praise. You have just 'broken out into a small group'.

Award yourself a fiver.

END OF INTERMISSION

Scandals and Disasters

Including:

- **Ballet and the KGB**
- **Scandal at the House**
- **Sorry, that is the rule – it's more than my job's worth**
- **The power of the computer**
- **The crazy world of finance**
- **Censorship**
- **A short history of fashion and the arts (inc. some technological developments!)**

Ballet and the KGB

KGB are the Latin letters for the Russian abbreviation for Committee for State Security (or as they say, *Komitet Gosudarstvennoy Besopasnosti)* which served as the Soviet Union's secret police, security and intelligence agency from 1954 to 1991. We begin with a political scandal, as much of the rest of this chapter involves itself one way or another with money. In the heady days of 1961 when Yuri Gagarin had just made the first manned space orbit, the Soviet Union was feeling pretty pleased with itself. One of its brightest young ballet stars, the 23-year-old Rudolf Nureyev, was on tour with Leningrad's Kirov ballet to western Europe. On completing their engagements in Paris, the troupe was waiting at Le Bourget airport when Nureyev made a break for freedom and hurled himself at a group of French policemen (who had previously been warned to expect him!), demanding asylum with the words:

'I want to be free'!

The Russians were not pleased, but there was little they could do there and then. However, back in Leningrad one of his friends was immediately removed from university and not even allowed to sit her finals. Rudolf was engaged to dance in the Paris-based Marquis de Cuevas Company. When he took the stage for the first time he was greeted with boos, jeers and coins and bottle tops being thrown on the stage. The KGB had arranged a 'claque' – this refers to an organised body of professional applauders and comes from the French for 'clapping'. Well known to the Romans, it was developed in modern times by the 16th century French poet Jean Daurat. Buying a number of tickets for a performance of one of his plays, he gave them away in return for a promise of applause. It could work the other way – those who did not pay the claquers had their performances spoilt by abuse! His talent and popularity soon put paid to this, but an East German friend who had returned to Berlin from Leningrad was harassed. Nureyev urged him by telephone to make his escape to West Berlin. He hesitated – and shortly afterwards the Berlin Wall was erected. He never managed to leave East Germany and died in unexplained circumstances at the age of 37. Research has now thrown up evidence that one of the plans devised by the KGB was to have Nureyev's legs broken. The only reason they did not do this was probably because the outcry would have caused them to lose the propaganda war – not because they suddenly had a softening of heart!

Bronislava Nijinska danced with the Mariinsky Ballet for three years but felt compelled to resign after the dismissal of her brother Vaslav Nijinsky chiefly because of the increasing fame of his performances in Paris. As a result of this she was deprived of her rights to the title 'Artist of the Imperial Theatres' and its associated income. It was generally accepted that she and her family left the Soviet Union in 1921 to visit her brother Vaslav in Vienna. His health had been deteriorating, but she had known about this in 1920. However, recent research describes a different and suppressed reason. The Cheka, (as the Soviet security police was then called) was stepping up its harassment of her and the students at her dance school, which they forced to close in 1921. During the following weeks she quietly made plans to leave, travelling west under false pretences, assisted by other dancers. After bribing the Soviet border guards, they waded across the River Bug into Poland.

Scandal at the House

It is probably only a small proportion of our readership who managed to listen to a Radio 4 broadcast in September 2007 when five leading lights were interviewed about the events involving the Royal Opera House (ROH) in the eighties and nineties. No doubt whole books could be written on the subject, but here is a summary of the interesting bits. Those interviewed were Deborah Bull, creative director of ROH2, Sir Jeremy Isaacs, general director 1988–1996, Nicholas Page, director of opera 1993–1998, Chris (now Lord) Smith, culture secretary 1997–2001 and the architect Jeremy Dickson.

By the end of 1997 the ROH, which had been closed for renewal six months before, was the subject of a scathing report from the Department of Culture, Media and Sports Select Committee i.e. the Government. The charges levelled were that there was an 'arrogance and presumption in its management and use of public money' and the recommendation was that not only the Chief Executive but also the whole board of managers should go. Heady stuff indeed. Let us go back a little further and see what had been happening to lead to this damning indictment.

First, let us set the scene. The seventies was a decade of great change and unrest in Britain as old industries such as coal, steel, ship-building and car assembly became ever less competitive on the world market. Industrial disputes seemed never-ending, and inflation tore away at savings and caused ever increasing wage demands. Clearly anything depending on money from the State was in for a hard time, and prey to barbs such as those penned by Simon Jenkins, *Sunday Times* Arts Correspondent:

> '...the ravenous Arts lobby, with its craven dependence on the State'.

Nevertheless, the ROH was located in the centre of Covent Garden – a busy fruit and vegetable market, in an old building desperately in need of basic maintenance such as rewiring in order to make it safe for the public. There was an appeal for funds in 1979, which HRH Prince Charles supported and became patron. Against this, critics pointed out that the ticket prices were some of the highest in the world, that opera singers could earn £5,000 a performance (which in those days was a reasonable *annual* salary!) and that productions were becoming increasingly lavish and expensive.

To be fair to ballet, Deborah Bull pointed out that far fewer expensive guest artists were employed and the ballet was run on a much tighter budget and seemed to get less public criticism because of this or, as she said, 'historically had a gentler ride'. Even today, ballet prices at the ROH are just about half of that for the opera. Although places for either can exceed £200, there are many at lower prices, sometimes because the view is limited but sometimes sold at the last minute or under various schemes to encourage, for example, the young. Before one jumps immediately to the idea of elitism and pricing out the 'ordinary person', just think what it costs to watch a football match.

During the 1980s the Arts Council subsidy under Lord Gowrie gradually diminished and in 1985 it was only through the generosity of a private benefactor that a damaging strike by the ROH orchestra was settled. In days of high inflation, wages did need to rise as their buying power was constantly being eroded.

By 1996 it was considered that a fly-on-the-wall documentary by the BBC (entitled *The House*) could do no harm as things were as bad as they could get, and, by showing the public what hard work and effort went on, both on stage and behind the scenes, public sympathy might be won, or at least public apathy countered. There is such a thing as bad publicity, and editorial content was not controlled by the ROH. The BBC naturally wanted to make a programme series that would be watched – private acts of hard work and dedication in these circumstances always come second to tantrums – no matter how rare and how out of context they may be taken. In the financial year of 1996 the ROH had not only reduced its deficit but had balanced its books – but this was not put into the documentary. It seems to be agreed that the National Lottery saved the day, though whether a capital city, and a centre of finance, culture, etc. such as London could have ever actually let its Opera House wither away is debatable. A grant of £55m was made with a further £23m to follow, to the accompaniment of newspaper headlines such as 'Greedy Beggars' Opera', 'Placido de Bingo', 'Pava Lottery'. The Labour MP Tony Banks claimed that the East End of London had in comparison only received £24,000.

The ROH was restored, expanded, integrated into its surroundings (the key phrase which repeatedly comes up is 'made accessible') and is a joy to visit. JB carps on about the price of programmes, ice creams, etc. but often goes to performances there. And really, if he didn't moan about something…

Perhaps now might be an appropriate time to insert a small guide to cost-cutting for those with children, grandchildren, godchildren and the like. The ingratitude of youth can perhaps be countered by the methods employed by one grandfather who wrote to his many grandchildren announcing that they should send him their thank you cards *before* Christmas. He had got so fed up of sending presents with never so much as an acknowledgement that he wrote that the best thank you letter would win a prize of £50. The runners up would get £10. Those who wrote nothing would get nothing. One is reminded of the writing of PJ O'Rourke:

> 'Everybody wants to save the world but nobody wants to help mother do the dishes.'

There is now a special interactive section – the reader becomes the writer! Take this along with you to the next performance.

The Arts must be subsidised – they are part of education.

Arguments for and against:

....

....

....

....

Taxes are raised from the hardworking public – they are to be spent on schools, hospitals and the like.

Arguments for and against:

....

....

....

....

What fun and arguments will ensue in the interval!

Did you find that a little difficult? Did JB's persuasive arguments, honed during a lifetime of barrack-room lawyer duties, overwhelm you? We thought so. So here is a little more information, which is all the more welcome if you are actually holding this argument, or filling in the above spaces, during an interval at the Royal Opera House.

What was not fully appreciated by the public, and is still not well known, is that this was not simply a refurbishment of the House – rewiring, repainting etc (although that renewal was essential) – but a redevelopment. The one-acre site became two and a half, with a whole street disappearing from the London street map. The new House has ten floors, six above stage level, four beneath, and the adjacent Floral Hall was jacked up four metres from ground level and another theatre stage built underneath. Half of the Floral

Hall, which now serves as restaurants, bars and the like (and is also used for concerts and tea dances) was dismantled to be sent away to be used as a market elsewhere. The space created is used for properties and rehearsals, thus bringing onto one site facilities which had been scattered around London. What an advance and what a wonderful stride in efficiency.

But it gets better. The Floral Hall now goes under the name of Paul Hamlyn – and the House became £10m better off as a result. We can sense an air of languidness descending over the reader and the phrase 'so what?' approaching the lips. Well, stay with this just a moment or two longer.

Prior to redevelopment, there were twenty productions per annum and the stage sets had to be removed by shifts of hands working through the night. They had to be built and dismantled as they stood. Now there is a system of wagons, each corresponding to a 15 by 5 metre section of floor. These are moved as a whole, a 60-ton sound-proof door being opened to allow them to be transported into assembly areas. A complete ballet set can be changed in two hours and no night shifts are needed. The number of productions has been doubled. Now, if only British Leyland had spent its subsidy so wisely….

You would be upset if there was no scandal, and we can give you just a little one, albeit an environmental one and not of the Royal Opera House's doing. Sets are kept in storage when not required and transported on lorries in a 'container' system – 15 metres once again coming to the fore. The whole lorry is driven into the House and raised on a lift so that its contents can be removed in one action. Where's the scandal? – it seems like a tremendously efficient way of doing things. And so it is. But because of the appalling transport system, it is easier to have the storage facilities in Wales and bring the lorries into the capital along the M4 motorway than on some reclaimed land close by. And that is a scandal.

Sorry, that is the rule – it's more than my job's worth.

'Latecomers will not be admitted'.

There must be many reasons for starting late – and just like with the railways, most of them are probably pretty amusing. The difference is that unlike with the railways and their tales of woe: the wrong sort of snow, leaves on the track (in autumn – who would have credited it!) etc. we are very rarely told. This really is an irony – British Rail and its successors imparting more information than is to be found elsewhere. A further irony is that JB was patiently waiting for a ballet to begin by reading an article about how in Peru the government was announcing (at a meeting where the official representative was himself late) that henceforth the country would try to adhere to 'English time' i.e. punctuality, rather than 'Spanish' – where everybody arrives late. Where is the irony in that? Well, it was a flamenco performance at Sadler's Wells. It started fifteen minute late – and only lasted just over an hour.

Row D, Sir?

Yes, that is just 8 rows from the front!

This may seem strange at first. The rows are labelled alphabetically and so the tickets we have bought should be rather nearer than that – D being only four from the start of the alphabet. But this fails to take into account the custom of labelling the first few rows AA, BB. Bras seem to be classified like that as well, and the connection is not really very clear. It is a bit of a mystery really why they bother naming the rows at all. The letters are tiny and on the floor, the seat numbers are minuscule and at first sight appear to be in Braille. Together with the low lighting found in most auditoria, this leads to the essentially proper first act of any performance which is, of course, the audience bobbing about, squeezing past each other, apologising to all and sundry and stepping on each other's feet. We would have it no other way. While we are about it, we might as well tell you that, at least at the newly refurbished Royal Opera House, all the seats have the same dimensions – unlike those to be found on aeroplanes and some other venues. Only those very high up which are sold more cheaply are slightly narrower. This is on the presumed basis that more places can be fit in, and the poor are thinner (the second assumption is not actually correct, but JB was never consulted). The most inexpensive seats are often referred to as 'the slips' – it was not worth printing a ticket for these – one simply received a slip of paper.

Even venues where the seating is not so rigid do not avoid the problem of the 'phantom rows'. A neat twist to this problem occurs at one (nameless) theatre where I, along with many others, book tickets. We carefully specify the **front** row, which in this case does actually happen to be A. So far so good. I have even been along and collected the ticket from the box office, confirming it is the front row. But then when you enter the auditorium, you find that the ticket sales have gone rather well. So well in fact that they have made another row comprising loose chairs (I don't know how they get around the fire regulations) and called 'AA'. So you are now sat behind some late ticket purchaser, your legs impossibly cramped and your view obstructed. Typically the box office bleat, 'There is nothing we can do!' Well, for a start they could rename row A the new AA and make the row of chairs which is now the front row A. At least when you have bought tickets for A and are expecting to sit at the front you are actually not behind anybody. Latecomers who bought tickets for the extra row can sit behind. The reader is invited to ponder on the following:

> *Being late is also a form of theft because, while you're taking extra time for yourself, the people who were on time are forced to wait and are robbed of minutes that cannot be claimed back.*

The power of the computer

Why is it that when you want to buy a holiday or whatever over the internet, or an extremely costly item in some expensive 'designer' boutique, you can make the purchase with your credit card – AND THAT IS IT! Yet when you present yourself in person to the ticket office at Sadler's Wells, the posh new Cardiff Millennium Theatre (and probably other venues as well), then that is not enough. 'The computer' has to have your address. You carefully explain that you do not want to be put on a mailing list, and hope that the rest of the queue (which is getting pretty impatient by now) and the rest of the staff are not tipping off their accomplices that you are at the ballet and not at home. They disarmingly reply:

> *It is not for junk mail, but for our records – it can be deleted immediately.*

Which poses the question, then why bother at all? This merry verbal tug of war continues until you wearily give in and probably give a false address. It is just one of those things we will probably never understand. JB's mucker, muse and mentor J reminds us all of the dangers of contactless credit cards. There is a temptation to casually swipe a credit card over the machine without looking at the figures. In unscrupulous restaurants this can have been tapped in incorrectly and is a devil of a job to rectify. It is also wise to always retain the receipt slip. The need for an alibi rarely arrives with warning and usually at the most inconvenient time. This advice was not given by J but by JB's more shady friends.

'The computer says no' is the other irritating power these machines have over us. When the computer says 'no', then nothing further can be done. This was experienced by JB in Madrid when a performance had been advertised as starting at 7pm. I got to the box office a few minutes before 2 that afternoon, waited while the couple ahead tried to buy a ticket with a credit card (it sounded like they were having the same problem as described for Sadler's Wells), then approached the window, to have the curtain drawn smartly to in front of me. It had struck 2pm. The man had finished his shift. I managed to shout through whether there were still tickets available and was told to come back later. I returned just after 6.30 pm to join a few other people milling about. The man was nowhere to be seen. Eventually he was retrieved from the front of the foyer. He explained that the performance began at 6.30 and not 7.00 as advertised and that the computer would not allow him to sell any more tickets – even though latecomers were still being admitted. And let's face it, the performance had probably not even started (see the section devoted to this). I explained the situation to the senior ticket salesperson and was eventually referred to the House Manager. I explained I would willingly pay for a ticket and be admitted during the interval (it was *Coppélia,* and I felt I could probably pick it up – and I was leaving Madrid the next day). Oh this was impossible, without a ticket, etc. But I couldn't buy a ticket. The computer said 'no'. After some gentle questioning about whether his theatre was in receipt of government or European Union funding (often a good ploy) he dramatically announced I would be let in during the interval FREE OF CHARGE. The theatre was about one-eighth full. So let us now turn to the whole question of finance and subsidy, etc. in a controversially titled section 'The crazy world of finance'.

The crazy world of finance

Let us just set the scene with a few examples of craziness, not from the world of ballet. Athena posters made more profit from their sale of pictures of the Countach sports car than Lamborghini ever did from making the actual vehicle. A bottle of water, produced locally and hardly taxed, costs more than the equivalent volume of petrol. An author scribbling away in his garret producing a novel which is at long last published (and how many ever are?) may well look askance at the asking price in the shops (and remember, the writer only gets a small part of this) compared with what is charged for the programmes at a theatre or ballet. And they are full of adverts!

The average audience for a ballet is predominantly female, a point which seems to be lost on those giving advice as to how to lead a successful life. You know who we are talking about – the counsellors, lifestyle consultants, etc. whose only point in common seems to be their own lack of success in the very things about which they purport to be experts. They neatly get around this by claiming that these failures have given them the experience to give (sell) others the benefit of their knowledge. Anyway, this is a digression. The important thing is that none of them seem to have cottoned on to the fact that just as the party has become the native fertility dance of the western world, ballets must be wonderful venues to meet members of the opposite sex – more particularly for men/boys to meet women/girls. Just as coffee bars in the nineteen fifties were never really just about drinking coffee, and discotheques in the sixties through eighties were only peripherally concerned with dancing, the current obsession with gyms is not really about fitness. How many people actually break out into a sweat? Apart from when they cannot find that cute headband from last week or have misplaced the new body lotion so expensively bought. They are all part of the elaborate mating ritual where posing, strutting and all the other elaborate aspects of the modern courtship ritual are practised. The ballet is perfect for this and it only needs some of the pony-tailed advertising men to get with the programme and market it. Remember you read it here first!

If you can remember back to the previous section, we were talking about the power of the computer and how it wouldn't allow JB into a performance which had not yet begun, but for which sales had finished. There were twenty-one dancers – and of course lighting, costume, front of house, etc. Fortunately they were only dancing to records – had there been an orchestra then the number of employees would have exceeded the paying customers. I counted these to be seventy-nine – this wasn't difficult as I estimated the stalls to comprise 600 and they were dotted about – it was, of course, impossible to work out how many were friends and relatives rather than true members of the public paying their way out of taxed income. In pursuit of more accuracy (the reader will be aware that no trouble is too much), I asked the manager. He said the venue's capacity was 595 downstairs (I hadn't been far off) and 200 in the circle, and he thought ticket sales had been 100. So there we have it – the place was one eighth full – on a Saturday in Madrid. Good grief! – on a Tuesday in the provinces it might only need a few taxis rather than a bus to bring the audience! I later found out that the subsidy was running at about 50%.

In a remarkably transparent review, except of course it was written in German (*Berliner Morgenpost* 24 March 2009) the annual amount for each venue per ticket sold by that venue was given. To this reader every figure seemed eye-wateringly high considering that this is the amount of money in euros per single ticket. At the lower end comes Friedrichstadt-palast €29. This is a very popular city centre venue showing very widely advertised music and dance reviews. At the other end of the spectrum at the highest is the Rundfunk-Orchester €199, closely followed by Staatsoper €185 then Komische Oper €167 then Deutsche Oper €156. One wonders if such revealing figures presented in such an open way would ever be readily available in the British press.

Subsidy, like inheritance, is usually wasted. Neither is earned – and rarely deserved. Contrast the heavily subsidised 'sales' person (See 'Computer says no') with your own personal observations of workers in other fields of endeavour. It is public money – but it is not really for the public at all! It is for the artistic 'insiders' – the Arts Industry – those who live off the taxes of the workers. They are not the only ones, of course – many of us do exactly the same thing – as any doctor working in the National Health Service is only too aware. There must be a certain stewardship of the taxpayers' money – the doctor, nurse, teacher, policeman have to put up with shortages. Demands on them are almost limitless, yet their budgets tight. How different this seems to the highly subsidised 'Arts'. Companies which play to venues half full (half may be a generous euphemism), yet schools are overcrowded. Art Galleries often resemble the good ship Marie Celeste just after somebody looked at the cabin wall planner and realised (too late) that the crew had all booked their holiday for the same time.

The problem is that ballet and the organisation needed to support it can be very expensive. Just glancing through a programme for Birmingham Royal Ballet, one finds that there are three finance officers and one finance assistant. In the department labelled

'Communications' there are thirteen people (two currently on maternity leave). Amongst the dancers there are six principals and six first soloists. One wonders whether they have got the proportions right, but they are the experts, so they must know, surely?

In deference to specialist knowledge it may well be that the following announcement has more than paid for the costs in terms of publicity – it was, after all, reported in the *Daily Mail* on 28 Feb 2022. The Royal Opera House is to hire an intimacy coach so that performers can shine on stage in sex scenes. It refers in fact to the opera (Handel's *Theodora*) about a Christian martyr forced into prostitution. One singer described the appointment as a 'relief for the singers'.

Compare that to the local hospital. People are ill, lying in bed day in day out and prone to infection, yet the washing facilities usually compare very poorly with museums – as do the lighting, floor covering, ambience, etc. etc. But these are just ordinary people – the worker bees, the drones. Not the highly sensitive aesthetic queen bees who have the ear of the Lottery or can fill out a well-turned plea for subsidy.

Feel free to fill the spaces below with counter arguments – you know you have many!

Counter arguments

....

....

....

Censorship

We now turn our attention to the thorny subject of censorship. Within the world of ballet this is less likely to involve such issues as politics, as might be found in the written word, but the question of how fully clothed (or not) a dancer might be does sometimes exercise the minds of the obsessive do-gooder. The sort of person who tirelessly works on behalf of others who, presumably in their eyes, cannot do this for themselves. The problem does not arise very often, but there are some ballets where the dancers, for the sake of the role, are dressed in a way which such people find upsetting. The rain forest people (man, wife and child) in *Still Life at the Penguin Café* spring to mind. This ballet is a sequence of vignettes of endangered species – and of course the rain forest people fall into this category. Would it be appropriate (or even sensible) to clothe them in anything more than what is regularly seen at any normal beach? Kurt Weill and Bertolt Brecht's *Seven Deadly Sins* has the principle visiting cities across American (it was written in 1933), encountering a new sin in each and becoming more and more corrupted. Just what would appropriate dress be? How corrupting are flashes of underclothes? Remember, in the narrative Anna ends up selling her body for financial gain, and if you don't want your children to see this, then don't bring them. Similarly do not attend yourself if you are going to be offended. But if you are, then it would probably be wise never to open a tabloid newspaper to page three, where there are static pictures of topless women!!!! Such a sight is far more daring than anything likely to be found at the ballet and would probably cause a stroke. But these busy-bodies don't seem to complain about things like this – probably because they would be onto a loser if they did – but give them the theatre and there is no stopping them.

It is amazing how people can see things that are not actually there, or jump to the wrong conclusions. JB had the job of organising outings at a hospital he was working in during his period in Germany. What better, then, than hire a minibus to go to Hanover and visit the Herrenhausen Gardens. In the Gartentheater there, a ballet company was putting on *Reise nach Kythera* (mus. Debussy, chor. Schindowski). The flyer was duly circulated, names collected, the bus booked and a picnic organised. The opening scene scandalised many of the group (which consisted almost exclusively of female nurses and one male doctor (JB) as those were the days when, particularly in the military, things were like that). Why were they scandalised? One of the cast members, in a static role, was topless. She was representing a nymph. This wasn't Shakespeare! What were they doing? JB had great difficulty understanding where Shakespeare had come into the argument at all. And then it finally dawned. Although the title had been clear and the format, i.e. ballet, had been clear – these people, because it was set in the park, had thought they were coming to see *A Midsummer Night's Dream* – as produced in Regent's Park, and which many had already seen. Some were quite disappointed. So there we have it – no matter what care is taken, misunderstandings will happen, people might be shocked or offended, and disappointment ensues.

Pantomimes seem to be bearing the brunt of pressure from political correctness which is threatening the centuries-old tradition of a Christmas romp. Traditional favourites such as *Robinson Crusoe* and *Sinbad* have been all but abandoned by producers, who fear that the depiction of 'natives' and 'cannibals' will cause offence on race grounds. Tony Gibbs, Chief Executive of the National Operatic and Dramatic Association, said the ever-sensitive issue of race was encouraging the organisation's members to 'play safe'. As he said in an interview (*Daily Telegraph* Monday 26 Nov 07):

> *'There is a dilemma between the need to stereotype villainous characters for ease of identification and the fear of vilifying someone because of their race.'*

Many panto performers are now beginning to censor themselves. *Aladdin* is becoming one of the hardest ones to do because of Abanazar's role as an Arabian villain. Following a production of *Snow White* in Truro, there was a serious exchange of letters in the local paper with an audience member who was angry that dwarfs had been used in the show. He said that it was demeaning and that jockeys should have been used instead. The reply came that that would be demeaning to jockeys. The Disney film studios are remaking their 1930s cartoon *Snow White and the Seven Dwarfs* (which of course is based on the 1812 fairy tale from The Brothers Grimm). To avoid giving any offence the dwarf characters are being 'reimagined to avoid reinforcing stereotypes'. In fact, in 2020 Disney began slapping racism warnings on some of its most iconic films, including *Peter Pan* and *The Jungle Book*. This is to alert viewers to sensitive scenes as it believes some of its older cartoons contain 'outdated racial or ethnic stereotypes'. It reads: 'This programme includes negative depictions and/or mistreatment of people or cultures' (*Daily Mail* 26 Jan 2022, and also reported on BBC Radio 4 *Today Programme*). However, the same newspaper (in an article illustrated with a photograph) announced under the title '*Braving The Rain*', 'swimmers jump into an outdoor pool'.

Staff involved with a school pantomime production of *Goldilocks and the Three Bears* posted a message on the theatrical website 'Amdram', asking whether they should keep the script's reference to 'those gipsies' in what the school describes as these 'you gotta be careful' days. Producers are also wary of including anything that may be too sinister or frightening, particularly in shows such as *Hansel and Gretel* and *Babes in the Wood*, which have scenes where children are abducted. In a production of *Jack and the Beanstalk*, the Giant will kidnap the village's livestock rather than the children. One cannot help but be reminded of the saying:

> *The situation was not broken beforehand, but it certainly was after it had been fixed.*

Britain's health and safety culture is also making an impact with some performers who fear their on-stage slapstick could expose them to legal action. The producers of *Peter Pan* in Cornwall had to do battle with health and safety officers who wanted the children in the audience to wear hard hats during the flying scenes. In Preston, audiences were told that the performers must not throw sweets at the children in case someone got hurt.

Some Medical Asides

Including:

- **Breathing**
- **Obese, well-built, anorexic**
- **Orthopaedic considerations**
- **The question of balance**
- **Motherhood**
- **The female athletic triad**
- **The question of noise**
- **I'll just carry on**
- **Tuberculosis**
- **Ballet and dentistry**

Studies in Performance Science at the University of Wolverhampton revealed that dancers have a huge incidence of injury. It seems that 80% have at least one injury a year affecting their ability to perform. In comparison, the rate for footballers and rugby players is 20%. Dance UK, in partnership with the Olympic Medical Institute of the University of Wolverhampton, are looking into this. At this point, a disclaimer is in order: the following chapter is not designed to provide medical advice or substitute for any form of professional help. It is simply, as explained in the title and foreword, an insight into some of the aspects of the world of ballet which might not be apparent to the average member of the audience. It will be apparent to the reader that JB's experience of medical practice in the United States has made him a somewhat cautious individual, particularly where litigation may be involved!

Time spent teaching at two American universities (University of Texas Medical Branch and Southern Illinois University, in case you are interested – thought not!) has also revealed that many people (especially teenage boys) when reading anything to do with medical aspects of life will be primarily interested in one thing. It would therefore seem sensible to start with this.

Research shows that the waist-hip ratio is important when we consider how attractive a woman is. European men prefer those with 0.7 – i.e. the waist is 70% that of the hip circumference. It varies between cultures, but western icons, no matter what their body weight, seem to follow this rule. So a 25-inch (65.5cm) waist matched with 36-inch hips should be the right proportions to carry off a seductive swagger – others might have to resort to high heels to achieve the same effect. It seems that women walk in a different manner according to their menstrual cycle. Women who are ovulating tend to walk with smaller hip movements and with their knees closer together (according to writers for the journal *New Scientist* – when JB was publishing research we never seemed to get support for topics such as this!). When men are shown recordings, they rated those in the less fertile part of their cycle as having the sexiest walks. This seems to contradict most other forms of mating behaviour and the answer lies in distance. Evolutionary sense dictates that it benefits a woman only to advertise her fertility to a man who would make a suitable mate. But men can pick up on the attractiveness of a woman's gait from afar – it can therefore act as an unwitting signal to less appealing males she may not want to choose. For closer encounters, research from the University of Aberdeen has demonstrated that a direct smiling gaze from a potential mate makes that person up to eight times more attractive. Looking away or to one side significantly reduces your chances. So take note, moody adolescents with your nonchalant sideways glances which you think make you look so cool. This gets you nowhere. Perhaps this is just nature's way of keeping down the rate of teenage pregnancy.

Breathing

To start off with the medical aspects of dancing it might well be a good idea to consider breathing. While sitting at rest the reader can be aware of various movements and muscles involved during quiet breathing and then contrast this with violent exercise. There are a variety of analogies used to explain how air is drawn into the body, the most common being that of bellows. The lungs are enclosed within the framework of the rib cage with the floor being formed by the muscular diaphragm. As the rib cage is expanded by pull of muscles, air is drawn in (inspiration), with the reverse happening on contraction (expiration). The rib cage may be likened to the firm outer surface of the bellows, but after this the analogy falls down when one considers the lungs – they are not empty cavities like balloons but more like sponges, with an interior consisting of a myriad of tiny muscular compartments giving them an elastic quality used in expiration.

In summary, inspiration requires a positive effort by the muscles controlling the chest wall to pull out the lungs and open up their interior. This creates a negative pressure which pulls air in from the outside and forces it out due to their elastic quality. Quiet expiration is just simple relaxation of muscle, with the elastic lungs doing the work, but for deeper and more forceful breathing muscular activity is added.

What about the muscular diaphragm? Contraction in inspiration increases the volume of the chest, but the volume of the abdomen below cannot be reduced to compensate – space can only be found by relaxation of the abdominal wall. This is known as abdomino-diaphragmatic respiration. In normal daily living both aspects of breathing, thoracic and diaphragmatic, run together in roughly equal proportions (although this varies from person to person). However, diaphragmatic breathing can (for no apparent reason) be reduced to virtually zero in many people and this is more frequent in women. Girls before puberty show the same full diaphragmatic breathing as boys, but after this many less active women change to primarily thoracic respiration. Dance requires good respiratory efficiency requiring a balance between both forms of breathing. There is usually a general lift and expansion of the chest wall when an average person takes a deep breath. A dancer requires these muscles for dance since much of the control of the arms comes from here. When a dancer requires an elegant extension of the spine the thoracic curve is reduced and this in turn creates some lift in the rib cage, requiring the dancer to focus on expansion of the lower chest on inspiration. Put simply, the requirements of dance use parts of the body which the non-dancer can dedicate to deep breathing.

Now that wasn't too bad, was it? Not too many long technical words. But let us take this slowly and not dive headfirst into too many of the complexities of orthopaedics. Instead, we have:

Obese, well-built, anorexic

In an aptly titled piece 'Small world cannot cope with larger people', it was reported that there were problems in the American theme park Disneyland. As passengers get ever more obese, the small boats which take people along past various tableaux are getting stuck and becoming grounded. This has got to such a state that by a particularly difficult S-curve a special platform has been built so that those 'with a fuller figure' can disembark.

We know that you are smiling to yourself about these foolish Americans with such little self-control that they cannot stop eating. But wait! Even our beloved Marks & Spencer is having to make changes from the previous size bra of a size G. According to the head of lingerie design, Soozie Jenkinson, there is a demand for bigger garments. Its best-selling cup size is 36C compared to 34B around five years ago. A quarter of bras sold by the chain are now DD cup or above, double the number of three years ago. Enter the mighty J-cup. This will be sold online as a trial before any decision is made to put them in stores.

Perhaps the New Zealand government will take heed, and use this as a screening tool. The wife of a submarine cable specialist (apparently a trade in short supply over there) was refused leave to join her husband who had already emigrated – she was considered too overweight. Robyn Toomath, speaking for 'Fight the Obesity Epidemic' and an endocrinologist, said she was opposed to obese people being stigmatised. 'However, the immigration department's focus is different,' she said. 'It cannot afford to import people into the country who are going to be a significant drain on our health resources.' One wonders just how carefully the decision 'overweight' was made. The Body Mass Index (BMI) measures a person's weight in relation to height. Anything over 25 is regarded as overweight, and 30 or above is obese. Researchers say less exercise, more calories and the side-effects of the contraceptive pill have combined to increase the average size of women's clothes from 12 in the 1950s to 16 today. For those of a mathematical bent there is a formula which can be used to calculate the BMI – otherwise a graph can be used with the heights and weights along the axes. The formula is: weight in kilograms divided by height in metres squared. For those still living in the world of imperial measurements it is: weight in pounds divided by the height in inches squared, with the final result being multiplied by 703.

With the current interest in 'size zero' models (clearly an American classification – Marilyn Monroe was reported in the British press to be a size 12) this has potential for a lot of problems. There was once a British Medical Journal Christmas edition article monitoring how tailors' dummies (the models found in shop windows) had become thinner during the course of the 20th century and that by the end women of such a size would have been too thin to menstruate. It was reported in the *British Medical Journal*, no less, (*Br Med J* 2008;337:839, which is the way references are written and drilled into JB when publishing medical papers!) that lap dancers earn more in tips when they are ovulating. The actual words used were 'scientists discovered that…', which may make you wonder just where all these research grants actually go.

It seems that dancers suffer from eating disorders such as anorexia more than any other group of people in any form of training or profession. The term 'anorexic' is used to describe someone with an abnormal attitude towards foods, and polls in America have reported them to be 1% of the population, mostly aged between 15 and 30. Of those, 6 to 10% would die as a result. We have seen earlier on how strict regulations (including regular and frequent weighing) can be found in ballet schools. Inevitably somebody who is on stage and in the public eye will (and must) have an awareness of their physical appearance. The problem occurs when there is a distorted image of the body and an intense fear of gaining weight, leading to the recognised psychiatric condition 'anorexia nervosa'. As has been amply demonstrated throughout the book, ballet is a demanding profession. It takes a strong student to deal with competition throughout training, auditioning and the rest and for those who already have insecurities and feelings of self-doubt, it is easy to understand how an eating disorder may develop. Knowledge, looking out for each other and awareness by teachers are key.

Well, this is the medical section, so now would be a good time to get back to something a little more medical and technical. The start will be gentle, with the least academic of the surgical specialties – orthopaedics.

Orthopaedic considerations

Eighty-five per cent of a dancer's flexibility is determined at birth – the genetic hand we are dealt. The remaining 15% may be improved by training and development of the muscles and joints. Like so much in life, and it seems particularly so in athletes, the sheer determination so beloved of Americans is not enough. Some are born to be great; others, no matter how hard they try, are just not up to it. This is no matter how much practice is put in. That is not to say that this is not important – it seems that it requires about 180 muscle repetitions for a movement to 'stick'. Imaging/visualisation is the term given to practice in your head, which might be helpful when one considers that in jumping, the joints experience forces up to fifteen times the body weight.

Followers of the television series *Downton Abbey* may be interested to learn that the actress who plays Lady Sybil, Jessica Brown Findlay, was all set for a promising career in ballet when, as she says in an interview for *The Sunday Times Magazine* (Oct 2011, p14-15) that her body let her down and she went through three operations on her ankles in her final year. The last one went wrong and on awakening after the procedure she was told that she would not be able to dance again.

Bone is the hardest living material in the body, with a rich blood supply and active cells (osteocytes) to maintain its functional integrity. Bone mass will keep increasing until the age of about 25 when a peak is achieved and bones are at their strongest. At about the age of 35 it begins to lose some of its calcium, with a more rapid loss being found at and after the menopause. Like muscle, bone responds to the stresses imposed upon it – a lack of work leads to calcium leaving and consequent loss of strength. This loss of calcium (osteoporosis) found in the unfit and elderly can also be seen in young dancers and athletes who have a poor diet or who are trying to reduce weight. In a way similar to the menopause, dancers who are amenorrhoeic (not menstruating) have lower levels of circulating oestrogen which can then lead to loss of bone strength and possible stress fractures. Even a period of rest can lead to a reduction in bone strength and the need for slow redevelopment not only of the muscles but the bones as well. When bones lose too much calcium their structure changes and the risk of fractures increases.

Bone growth is affected by puberty. In girls, bone growth slows down after puberty whereas in boys secretion of the male sex hormone testosterone usually leads to a rapid increase in bone growth. At first this is not matched by the controlling muscles or the brain's ability to cope with the increased limb length. This leads to the classic 'clumsy, gangling youth' until the brain and muscles 'catch up'. For girls, there are various theories about when pointe work in classical ballet should start, with arguments being made that bones are too weak until a certain age. Of far more importance, though, is the time at which she has developed adequate muscle control over her feet and body to give her the necessary strength. Bone forms rigid levers on which muscles act to produce movement, but there is another important component to the skeletal system – cartilage. This also contains living cells, but there is no direct blood supply (this comes via diffusion through the substance of the cartilage) and it is also without a nerve supply. Consequently it can be injured without producing pain, unless this comes indirectly from surrounding tissues. Due to its low metabolic rate it has a poor capacity for repair and so any injury may be permanent. Cartilage not only covers the load-bearing ends of bones but is found in the intervertebral discs between the bones of the back. A flexible sort is found at the ends of the ribs (the costal cartilages) and it is also found in the larynx, tracheal and bronchial rings and parts of the nose and ears. The function of cartilage within the joints is to give the bone a smooth hard surface which is also slippery – it is three times as slippery as smooth ice, being assisted in this by synovial fluid. With reasonably correct training patterns, stresses put upon the joint should not lead to cartilage damage in a healthy person. In classical ballet, turn-out is used to allow a wide range of movement at the hip joint. It has become fashionable to expect a flat turn-out as displayed by the feet. This is possible for dancers with a highly mobile hip joint and/or suitably directed socket. For others, the situation can be forced by developing a sideways twist at the knee. This produces a less controllable joint which increases the risk of lower leg injury and particularly cartilage ruptures.

The quadriceps group of muscles form the major part of the bulk of the front of the thigh and are vital for the knee joint's stability as otherwise it is an unstable joint. Two of the four muscles (quadriceps means four heads) give power to straightening the leg (extension) working through the kneecap (patella) as a lever, while the other two give support at the sides.

The thighbone (femur) and shin bone (tibia) are not in a straight line at the knee due to the upper end of the femur being set on the side of the pelvis at an angle. This angle is greater in a female due to the relatively wider pelvis. Pressure of the body tends to push the knee inwards (knock-knee) unless effectively controlled by the pull of the inner thigh muscles in support of the strong medial ligament of the knee joint. When the support is lax the knee is allowed to fall in to some extent – a risk greater in females due to their wider pelvis. In fact, a high proportion of the adult female population suffer from a degree of knock-knee. Poor control of knock-knee not only induces strain on the medial ligament but also induces rolling in of the foot. Such is the importance of quadriceps control over the knee joint that anybody who is laid up in a hospital bed for more than a short while is given daily quadriceps exercises. In addition, even a minor problem around the knee joint automatically leads to brain inhibition of muscle control over it with consequent loss of muscle power.

The ankle joint is a pure hinge joint designed to give support to the foot when standing. It has to take the full load of the body when standing. The bones of the ankle joint are much looser when rising onto pointe, jumping or landing. This requires good side (lateral) muscle control, which is largely unnecessary when standing. There are two lateral muscles running down each side of the ankle joint into the foot and they are also responsible for rotational movement there. On the inner side they produce inversion (from the dancer's point of view they are also prevent rolling in). The outside two muscles produce eversion. Clearly it is necessary to have a strong balancing muscle system which can give stability to the ankle when rising onto the toes. The only muscle group working purely on the ankle joint is that of the calf, which attaches to the back of the heel via the Achilles tendon. Using this lever, the muscles transmit enormous forces to flex the foot and lift it onto the toes as when walking, running or rising onto pointe. The classic case of an Achilles rupture involves a person engaging in sport more vigorously than current physical conditioning merits – the sort of person who plays sport infrequently or at the start of a fitness regimen is particularly vulnerable. When one realises that just walking involves forces to the foot equivalent to one and a half times bodyweight it is no surprise that jumping produces much more and can lead to injury leading to a weak ankle and a tendency to limp. Pain is often felt as a blow or kick to the lower leg. It may be accompanied by an audible click when rupture occurs, a phenomenon more often reported in textbooks than real life! However, it must be noted that the action of other flexor muscles of the foot ensure that even if it is completely torn, it may be possible to still flex the foot. Hence being able to walk does not rule out a rupture.

Ligaments are also especially important in the knee joint. While the quadriceps pull the knee into its firm straight state, it is the taut cruciate ligaments which produce the slight twist to lock the joint in extension. In a similar manner the thick broad medial and lateral ligaments are there to control the hinge activity and they should also remain taut. Lax ligaments are more likely to be damaged, such as may occur due to improper stretching, as so often happens in the knee from forcing a flat turn with potentially disastrous results. The ideal ballerina has toes which point outwards, the 'turn-out' being the cornerstone of classical ballet. It begins at the hip, moving down to the knee, shinbone, ankle and foot. If the leg is not turned out naturally it can be done by stretching and this takes its toll. In fact a forced flat turn-out is probably the cause of the highest proportion of both early and long-term knee disabilities in classical ballet dancers. This is best explained in the words of the late Dr Kenneth Backhouse OBE, former Surgeon Captain RNR and anatomist Royal College of Surgeons, a man not only of infinite wisdom but also patience (he tutored JB for the primary FRCS examination).

> *Turn-out is designed to allow freedom to maintain dance 'en face' and to free the range of the legs to the side and not to position the feet. It should arise purely from the hip joint.*

The question of balance

For most of us (at least when we are not drunk) balance is simply a question of not falling over, but it is far more important for the dancer who must be secure not only in posture but also in movement. The brain relies upon constantly receiving sensory information from the organs of balance (the inner ear), the eyes and muscle, tendon and joint sensibility. Regarding the eyes, we have all sat in a car or railway carriage and thought that we were moving when in fact it is the adjacent vehicle. The eyes are constantly recording movement of the body relative to fixed objects around. If the movement is too great and too rapid (as in a turn) then this fails. This of course is the important reason for spotting in turns. It is also the explanation for the phenomenon of how one can drink heavily and remain standing at the bar without any problems but the moment one returns home, closes the eyes and lies in bed the world starts to spin. This brings us to the second mechanism – that of the multitude of signals received from the sensation of the feet on the firm surface of the floor. Thirdly, and strangely enough the least important of the three basic mechanisms which maintain balance, are the organs of balance themselves. The reason dizziness is produced by ingestion of alcohol is that the alcohol seeps into the fluid of the organs of balance. It has a different specific gravity to the fluid there and this sets up currents which stimulate the nerve cells, giving a false impression of motion.

The feet are finely equipped with highly responsive pressure sensors. Nevertheless when standing upright there is always a small amount of swaying of the body as they add to the information on movement from the eyes and ears. On closing the eyes the range would increase considerably, even in a trained dancer. When a dancer raises to demi-pointe, the area of pressure reception is much reduced; on full point there is only pressure on the toe-tips, reducing the sensation from the soles of the feet to virtually nothing. In summary, dance produces disruption of all three of these important sensory controls of equilibrium. This would be unacceptable to an untrained person. The dancer must be aware of sensory limitations during training and develop a heightened sensory awareness and techniques such as 'spotting'.

It has also been found that dancers suppress signals sent to the brain. According to research done by Dr Barry Seemungal of London's Imperial College, who had a group of 29 ballet dancers and 20 rowers of similar fitness level being spun around in a chair in a dark room, for the dancers, the room seemed to stop spinning more quickly afterwards. Brain scans showed that the area of the brain that processes messages from the internal ear were smaller in them than in the rowers, implying the messages were being suppressed rather than utilised. In other words, it seems that it is preferable to rely more heavily on vision and joint position sense rather than the inner ear.

> *Stability training – the surprising exercise every over-50 should do to improve strength (and brain power) is often neglected – but it can be a vital aid to a longer, healthier life (Daily Telegraph 19 Feb 2022).*

This is the headline to attract the reader, but the article goes on to say that falls in later life are a frequent cause of prolonged health problems such as fractures, and a tremendous burden on health services. This risk is best prevented sooner rather than later by building stability in the legs and trunk. Public Health England specifically recommends Nordic walking as a balance improving activity – it also strengthens muscles and bones thanks to the added resistance provided by the poles. More sophisticated and exercises might involve a wobble board, but failing that one can simply practice standing on one leg and then the other.

Whilst considering the practice and acquisition of new skills, JB cannot help but be reminded of his experiences at conferences where doctors and lawyers are present (as part of his working with the Ministry of Justice, not because he is the subject of litigation himself). A surgeon will approach the dessert table of a buffet, push back his shirt cuff, take care that his tie does not trail into anything, select a knife, cut into a cake, meringue, cheesecake or whatever with two incisions, insert the knife under the wedge, flick it onto a plate and return to his table. A lawyer fiddles about, uncertain as to whether a large or small spoon, fork or knife would be best, whilst a queue builds up. He drips his tie into the fruit salad, half destroys whatever he is trying to cut in to which he then spills trying to lift it onto his plate. The scene has been repeated so often I do not find it funny any longer!

Motherhood

Anya Sainsbury CBE who danced with Sadler's Wells (later Royal) Ballet from 1951 to 1964 retired at 32 when pregnant with her second child. She had returned when her first baby was six months old, but, she states 'coming back after two – that was unheard of'. Dame Antoinette Sibley, who was one of the leading dancers of her generation, became a mother at 37. She continued dancing for three more years before retiring in 1978. Two years later, after the birth of her second child, she returned to the stage, finally retiring at the age of 50. Zenaida Yanowsky, who as a principal was doing 30 to 35 performances a year, stated that she was back on stage within three months of the birth of her son. This would seem to be a natural progression of pregnancy having less and less of a hindrance to a ballet career. However, she had other considerations, for example the particular role. Nicola Roberts had to stop work in her fourth month of pregnancy. As a soloist with The Royal Ballet she had been cast to dance one of the animals in *Tales of Beatrix Potter* and the role was too dangerous. 'I had to wear a mask (as part of my costume), which meant I couldn't see or breathe properly, and I had all these stairs to run up and down.' (*The Independent* 14 July 1994). The English National Ballet star Daria Klimentova was interviewed by *The Times* (13 Oct 2007) under the headline 'motherhood has made her a better mover'. She had a baby at the height of her career and, on answering the question as to whether motherhood changed her attitude to ballet, stated that she danced better and had more confidence with something else to focus on, so she was more relaxed.

The female athletic triad

JB is a surgeon specialising in diseases of the ear, nose and throat (ENT) so this draws heavily on the expertise of Dr Cathy Speed and an academic paper which appeared in the *British Medical Journal*. This is a remarkably erudite article, as befits a physician such as Cathy. There is a long-standing rivalry dating back to the mediaeval guild companies between physicians (who are clever and investigate and diagnose their patients) and surgeons (who are practical and treat and cure their patients!). It is the inverted snobbery of English surgeons which makes them forsake their 'Dr' title for 'Mr' – as they originated from the mediaeval Company of Barber-Surgeons. Dr Speed is not a gynaecologist, but a rheumatologist specialising in sports and exercise medicine. Her original work was too complicated for JB to understand at first (and even third!) readings. The salient features, rather than the whole heavily referenced academic piece, are given as follows:

> There is a risk, which is often not recognised, to sportswomen of exercise-related menstrual dysfunction and impaired bone health. The main underlying cause of the menstrual problems, which can range from luteal phase deficiency through failure to ovulate, scanty periods to full-blown lack of menstrual bleeding or failure of periods to begin at all, is suppression of the hypothalamus. This is a tiny gland in the brain which has a controlling function over many hormones. What causes this hypothalamic suppression? It seem that there is a variety of causes in sportswomen and they include the physical and psychological stress of training and competition, shortage of calories, low body mass and low body fat, and alteration in how hormones are metabolised. There may also be alterations in leptin values – this seems to be something that has been discovered since JB did his American Board exams (only a few years ago) and shouldn't worry the average reader. It certainly has not worried him and he has not been struck off yet for this

> oversight! The consequences of this suppression can include musculoskeletal injuries (in particular stress fractures), infertility and the general medical consequences of low oestrogen levels.

When menstrual dysfunction occurs in sportswomen in combination with a low bone mass and energy deficit, the syndrome is termed the 'female athletic triad'. What a relief to all! The physicians have collected a group of problems, put it into a 'syndrome', and given it a name! See the first paragraph about the difference between surgeons and physicians. So what does this all mean in practical terms? The energy deficit is usually related to eating disorders and is partly influenced by peer pressure, what is read in magazines and how youngsters see themselves. Many mistakenly think that they are overweight. Secondary amenorrhoea (i.e. the periods started normally but have then stopped – like when pregnancy occurs) can be found in up to 44% of women who exercise vigorously. This is the extreme, but more subtle menstrual disturbances are more common, occurring in nearly four-fifths of very active women. The impact of this on bone mineral density is unclear. So that is very helpful, isn't it? It has not been determined at what level of exercise the risk of menstrual dysfunction occurs (more helpful stuff here!), but 'management of exercise-related menstrual dysfunction aims primarily to restore normal menstrual cycles'. The advice is education of patients, coaches, peers and parents about the risk of excessive exercise in girls, together with dietary counselling. In other words, probably what any sensible grandmother would say.

A gynaecologist colleague who was a very slim woman and had probably never been to aerobics in her life relates that stress incontinence can be the result of too much of this activity if poorly supervised. Do bear in mind that it is part of the duty of a book which purports to talk about subjects not normally covered and not shy away from the difficult areas. For many female athletes in high impact sports like gymnastics or rugby a constant downward pressure is placed on the pelvic floor. This can occur to the extent where it becomes too tight, in contrast to other forms of incontinence where weakness is the problem. Training has damaged the way the pelvic floor's muscles contract. It is estimated that female athletes are 177% more at risk of developing pelvic floor issues and incontinence than sedentary women. The winner of the 2017 British National Championship in trampolining, explained (*Daily Mail* 23 Feb 2022) that it was common for gymnasts and trampolinists to have problems with their bladders as they are often putting 'up to 16 times their body weight' through the trampoline.

The question of noise

The background hum of a train averages 65 decibels – telephone ringtones come in at 78 decibels but an announcement on a train may reach 85 decibels (presumably so it can be heard above all those ringtones). 85 decibels is the level at the workplace that, if continuous, signals to the employer that he must take action to protect his employees. Even in parks, noise levels can be such that they never drop to a level which can be thought of as not intrusive. In other words, you may be able to read a few headlines in a newspaper, but not a book. The government considers that 57 decibels is the level for the 'beginning of community annoyance'. JB has attended venues when a small cough sweet has been left on each seat, serving not only to help with coughing but possibly also as a reminder to the audience to be quiet and avoid rustling paper etc. This was usually at opera performances rather than ballet but of course the principle applies to performances of any kind where there are quieter periods.

There are some disabilities which are exacerbated by the denial of the sufferer that anything is wrong. This is most often encountered in hardness of hearing. We start to lose the ability to hear high-pitched sound at quite an early age – estimates are in the early 20s. This progresses throughout life. In a similar manner, the lens of the eye hardens and small print becomes difficult to read. When our arms are not long enough for us to distance ourselves from small type, we revert to reading glasses. The wearing of glasses has always been associated with intelligence, in comparison to hearing aids. It is strange to think that a pair of spectacles balanced on the nose and reaching left and right across the whole of the face is worn without a second thought, but a whole industry has developed to make hearing aids more and more inconspicuous. They are sometimes so small that they are too fiddly to be worn with comfort or jam deep into the ear where they block the canal with wax. People might be a little reticent to use a walking stick to help with mobility and balance but as yet there do not seem to be any made of transparent material such as a clear plastic or glass to render them invisible. The best hearing aids are those with a good seal of the mould. This goes into the ear canal and should exclude outside sound to prevent feedback (that irritating whistle). A forward-facing microphone is best as the majority of sound will be from a speaker opposite the individual. It is a shame that deafness is regarded as something which has to be hidden. Somebody hard of hearing is best seated in a restaurant in a corner rather than the centre of the room surrounded by sound, and it is usually better to speak in a clear voice rather than a loud one.

I'll just carry on

It seems that whereas in the past one might have telephoned in sick, now, according to the Chartered Management Institute, we are more likely to turn up for work rather than stay at home to recover. This is possibly a reflection on the current economic climate and contracting job opportunities. The Institute's survey of 1,511 workers found that one in three 'is afraid to take time off from work when needed'. Despite this, another finding was that illness rates have gone up. There are two theories for this:

- as a population we are healthier – therefore we worry more about minor sniffles and aches which probably would not have been even noticed before
- many minor ills are a reflection of stress – the sort you get from years of hating your job.

A ballet dancer's career is notoriously short but, as always, there are exceptions. Frederik Franklin CBE, dancer, ballet master and director was born in 1914. He made his professional debut as a chorus boy in 1931 in a Casino de Paris revue starring Josephine Baker. His final performances were in a minor role of Friar Lawrence in Kenneth McMillan's *Romeo and Juliet* during July 2010; he died in 2013 aged 98. Such longevity is not confined to professional dancers. It was reported in *The Times* (12 Jan 2008) how 'Ballet dancer, 88, steps into the limelight', going on to say that after learning to dance at the age of 79, retired teacher John Lowe would perform in Prokofiev's *The Stone Flower* at the age of 88. He stated that: 'I practise each day and I have got a rope at home that I use to pull my leg up higher'.

Sometimes good fortune lends a hand, and this is perhaps best illustrated by the Rudolf Nureyev – Margot Fonteyn story. Following his escape from the Soviet Union in 1961 the 23-year-old Nureyev danced with the 42-year-old Margot Fonteyn, a situation she herself described as 'mutton dancing with lamb'. She was even mistaken for his mother in a restaurant! Their first dance together was *Gisele*, a role she had first performed in 1937. It was so successful it rejuvenated her career and he became her principal partner in The Royal Ballet.

But in reality, as we get older our bodies become less capable of managing feats which we were capable of in our younger years. This is perhaps most visible to an observer in loss of height and posture. In fact before the age of 70 there is an average height loss of 1 cm for every 10 years. The classic 'Dowager Hump' is the phenomenon often seen, but not confined, to elderly ladies. Loss in height and form of the vertebral bodies of the upper back lead to a tipping forward of the head and a stooped appearance. Degenerative disc disease is a bit of a misnomer, sounding as it does like a progressive, threatening condition. Strictly speaking it is neither degenerative nor a disease but a natural part of ageing. It affects us all but at various rates and in fact is present in 30% of 30 to 50-year-olds. Most do not develop symptoms. 'Degenerative' implies symptoms getting worse with age, but whilst the degeneration may progress as we get older, the resulting lower back pain tends not to get worse and in fact it usually gets better over time. So age does not necessarily mean we will all be popping pills but there is an inevitable loss of flexibility.

It is also recognised that with age our cardiovascular and musculoskeletal systems in general become less efficient. This is reflected in the various physical tests required by organisations such as the military, police force, etc. As we get older, our walking speed averages out to nearly 2 minutes per mile (1.2 min/Km) slower at the age of 60 compared with 20-year-olds. Of course this has little relevance unless walking speed is known. Compared to the acceleration 0 to 60 of motorcars and the like, this is far less widely known among the population at large.

How long do you think it takes to walk 100m? It is in fact related to age and sex, but a steady average walking pace is 1.65m/s – in other words it takes about one minute to walk 100m. A slow walking pace (as considered by HM Courts & Tribunal Service for benefits and the like) is 40-60m per minute and very slow would take more than a minute to walk 40m. That is all very interesting if you can picture 100m – it is the length of a football pitch. Something perhaps seen more often is a double-decker bus, which is 9.144m (or 30 feet). Bus aficionados need not write in – JB is well aware of the mini double-deckers to be found on some routes in West Yorkshire designed to go under low bridges, etc. Put another way, walking speed (as calculated by the Road Research Laboratory) in miles per hour is:

Males under 55	3.7	Males over 55	3.4
Females under 55	3.1	Females over 55	2.9

To complicate matters even further, this varies according not only to sex but also age, height, stride, fitness levels and associated diseases. But for our purposes, we will assume that the dancer is fit, length of stride is not going to alter, but with age things slow down!

Of course, wisdom and insight, patience and many other favourable qualities increase – as JB is finding. Let me give an example: no medical writing for the lay public should miss the important advice that should you find yourself an inpatient on a urology ward, do not tick the breakfast option of apple juice. Better safe than sorry,

Tuberculosis (TB)

The reader may well be (rightly) surprised to see this heading – after all, this is not a medical dictionary. But this disease, which may well be virtually unknown to or even unheard of by younger readers, has had a profound effect on the Arts. Medically speaking it had a profound effect upon the population, being a leading killer in 19th and early 20th century Europe before the development of effective antibiotics. Special tuberculosis hospitals were found in each city and a few years in a sanatorium with plenty of sunlight (both natural and artificial), beds out on open terraces, etc. was the lot of many who first presented with a persistent cough. This is the setting found in the original film *Alfie*, played by Michael Caine. But the question still burns – why bring it up here? Well, just as so much current literature depends on the suspicious wife finding a ticket or receipt 'while going through the pockets of the errant husband before going to the dry cleaners', and detective stories which hang on DNA evidence, so it was that in previous years tuberculosis was the hook on which the story revolved. It also took away many authors – in the 20th century alone Anton Chekhov at 44, Katherine Mansfield 36, D H Lawrence 44, George Orwell 46.

Other connections of TB to dance, literature and music include:

(You know the drill by now – here is one to start you off – *La Traviata* has the heroine (spoiler alert…) of tuberculosis)

……………………………………………………………………………

……………………………………………………………………………

……………………………………………………………………………

Ballet and dentistry

As far as is known, there are no associated ill effects from ballet on dental health, and for this helpful information we are indebted to Charles Bennett, BDS. He simply wanted a mention in the book and is the Honorary Dental Officer to the authors. JB's other brother is the Honorary Nursing Officer. It has always been their father Norman's regret that he didn't have useful sons like plumbers, electricians, painter-decorators who could do something practical around the house. It is amazing how many of the readers of the initial manuscript identified with this!

In a spirit of brotherly cooperation, it would be churlish to relegate Charles to a permanent position of Niles to my Frasier, so we are letting him have his very own little section. So, mother, you are always saying I could never share. Here we are. His own section. In my book.

Special section by Charles J C Bennett, BDS

My talented elder brother has always had literary ambitions and, being a salaried doctor, plenty of time to pursue his hobby. As a self-employed cosmetic dental surgeon, my writing is restricted to the cheque book and the main beneficiaries are the Inland Revenue, my ex-wife, my latest wife and my children.

There is, it has to be said, a certain snobbery which exists between similar professions – the medical and dental spring to mind – and to a certain extend this is also found in the world of dance.

The doctor, as I understand, has eschewed financial reward for the love and respect of the masses:

'What do you do?'

'Oh, I'm a doctor'

'How marvellous for you, such hard work, so unappreciated' etc.

A similar parallel may be made with ballet in comparison to other dancers. You think not? Well, witness the scene from the sci-fi disaster movie *Independence Day*. In an incongruous chance meeting following the destruction of the American White House, the First Lady is assisted by the hero's girlfriend (a stripper).

'You're the First Lady, aren't you?'

'That's right, and what do you do?'

'I'm a dancer'

'Ballet?'

'No, exotic'

'Oh, I'm sorry' (!!!)

There was a period a few years ago when there was a groundswell of opinion in the dental profession for practitioners to call themselves 'Doctor'. All manner of reasons were put forward, including alignment with current practice in Europe and the USA. Ego was never mentioned. Now a dentist calling himself a doctor is just an extreme case of hubris. A medical doctor's university training is longer (and the entrance requirements tougher), and postgraduate training more demanding. To my shame I would excuse myself when my patients asked why I did not use the title by stating that my esteemed brother is a doctor and it might prove confusing to staff and the like when messages were being relayed. The real reason was that I did not want to align myself to such a noble profession for fear that patients might expect my expertise to extend beyond teeth – and it also saves me from having to venture medical opinions. That is not to say that I would never be available for a medical opinion should the need arise. Several times when my nursing or reception staff have complained of 'women's problems' I have generously offered help, but qualified its value by stressing: 'I'm not a gynaecologist but I'll take a look'

Dentists, unlike doctors, do not crave professional respect or public adoration. A patient who is less distressed when paying the bill than when receiving treatment is more than enough reward for us. That is not unique to dentistry – repeat business to a lap dancer is more highly valued than a good review in the Arts Section of a quality daily newspaper. But, dear reader, do not concern yourself with the lack of respect our chosen professions endure. We do not need, or want, your pity. In fact, by foregoing these other rewards we do quite well for ourselves.

That is not to say that I do not hold my brother and his ilk in the highest regard – ditto the persevering ballet dancer whose career, like that of the doctor, is an arduous climb of self-improvement. It can at times make me feel a little remorseful – have I not exploited my talents enough by choosing dentistry? I do sometimes dwell on such imponderables as I drive home to my large house in the stockbroker belt in my Jaguar, or perhaps while watching the sunset at my place in the south of France – mmm, where did it all go wrong?

I could compare our careers to those of the dancing profession. The consultant NHS surgeon is the revered leader of a large team – like the prima ballerina of a large troupe. I am more likely to be compared to a dancer of the more exotic type i.e. the lap dancer. There are pros and cons. When my brother performs a brilliantly delicate piece of surgery, the patient and his family are unanimous in their praise of … the whole team: 'of course the surgeon did his job, but the nurses, the porters, even the cafeteria staff were all marvellous.'

In ballet terms:

> 'the prima ballerina was good, but the whole troupe made it the spectacular event that it was'.

If a calamity occurs, and this regrettably does sometimes happen, then the condemnation of the surgeon is absolute. But his staff are spared. So it is with the prima ballerina:

> 'the star was hopeless, but everybody else did a tremendous job'

Veneers – a shiny smile to dazzle and amaze

Where I practice, the ambition, it seems, of every young person is to have a tanned skin and white teeth. Sadly the reality is the direct opposite – hence the profusion of sunbed salons and cosmetic dentistry. But it is not natural to have brilliantly white teeth. In fact, current practice in the USA (where fashions seem to originate and then percolate through to Europe) is for a more natural, i.e. less than overall brilliant white, look.

You may or may not be aware that veneers are the name (strictly porcelain veneer in dental parlance) given to a restoration applied to the visible part of the front teeth to improve their appearance. Before being applied they seem delicate and flimsy but they are remarkably strong once correctly in place. I suppose the ballet analogy would be the delicate, flimsy-looking ballerina who, as we have learnt from earlier chapters, is a powerhouse of strength able to perform athletic feats which many an athlete would be proud to achieve.

As my knowledge of ballet is woefully inadequate I would presume that the normal colour of a ballerina's costume is white – so it used to be with veneers. People wanted white teeth and a perfectly even smile (we even called it the 'Hollywood smile') to match the unnatural appearance of our celebrities.

Now we find requests for slight malformations, defects and 'character' in their veneers to give the impression that they are not false. To muse philosophically, perhaps the overt falseness of a smile reflects society's embracing of culture which values appearance over achievement. Maybe an environment where stupidity is ignored (or even rewarded if a person's appearance is deemed acceptable) is the bitter pill we just have to swallow. If we continue to pray on insecurities by dangling the carrot of a better life, if only they match the style and behaviour of those celebrities they aspire to, then perhaps those large sums of money spent on achieving 'the perfect smile' are well spent. Just remember, success is not guaranteed.

I have spent many long fruitful years making Hollywood smiles. Now, as the public tires of the culture of celebrity, I am replacing those unnaturally bright white veneers with more 'naturally-looking' ones. It might be tempting to consider that the measure of a society's intelligence is inversely proportional to the proportion of unnaturally white teeth.

Appearance is of course important – but it is not overridingly important. Achievement does have its place and should also be given credit. Just think back to those interviews when celebrities are asked for a summary of recent events in their lives:

> 'I've had my boobs done, I've met somebody famous, I'm sleeping with somebody famous,' etc. etc.

Indulge me and follow this advice: check on the whiteness of their teeth. If you decide you might need to wear sunglasses, reserve judgement on anything they might say. Try not to listen to the siren-like calls of celebrity, avoid being sucked in and concentrate on those happier, simple times when gossip was malicious, spiteful and hurtful. It was spread by word of mouth and not celebrity magazines and reality television. How can you respect anyone who clearly has no self-respect?

So, all in all, my work concentrates on the appearance and is highly susceptible to personal opinion, the patient's mood, self-esteem, etc. For me, as previously stated, my job is like a lap dancer – primarily one on one (two on one if you include my nurse, but she is rarely praised or noticed) and satisfaction is DIRECTLY proportional to the amount of money spent. If you are not happy with the result you get your money back, try again or find somebody else – and unlike consultants or ballerinas, there are a lot of us about to choose from.

It occurs to me that I might seem to be too dismissive of the role of the dental nurse. It is true that the relationship between patient and dental surgeon largely excludes the ever-present dental nurse.

But, when the patient has gone then the perpetual sparring match between them resumes.

It has been said that a dental nurse is like a right hand to a dental surgeon. The nurse-dentist pas de deux is a wonderful sight to behold (I married my nurse – it was even worth my ex-wife's cries of 'I told you so!'). There is a soupcon of flirtation, a respect for each other's capabilities, mutual dependency – and an underlying resentment from both parties that the other is grossly overpaid for what little work they do.

I should imagine the same degree of resentment exists between the headlining ballerina and the succession of partners with whom she deigns to dance. Romeo and Juliet have nothing on the frissons of tension which exist when the dentist compliments or criticises his nurse. Only the timing is of consequence – a compliment is soon forgotten but a criticism remembered for an eternity, being dusted off and brought out at every wage review!

Nevertheless, whenever my esteemed brother is a (non-paying) patient, he makes up for his financial embarrassment by commenting on how well we work together. I am inclined to agree – we anticipate each other's moves much like a ballet duet. The interchange of instruments is comparable to a magician's sleight of hand; the range of emotions experienced during a day's work resembles high drama. Hidden behind our face masks, we communicate Roger Moore-like with arched eyebrows – as the patient's demands become ever more incredible our foreheads furrow in a breathtaking balletic display.

But the good nurse really comes into her own whenever a modicum of sympathy is needed during the course of treatment. Her maternal instinct soothes and comforts while the dentist fumes and tuts, begrudgingly respecting her role, privately thanking his lucky stars he doesn't have to do all this playacting. The impatient dentist is like the jealous Montague (or is it Capulet?) despairing at the affection his Juliet is wasting on Romeo. You see, it is just like ballet!

And when tragedy strikes, the nurse is there to alleviate the despair into which her master might sink. Although powerless to take away the pain, she does, I think (I hope) understand. And that helps. I refer of course to that dreadful moment which occurs from time to time in the professional life of all dentists – the day we undercharge a patient. The words

> 'Is that all, I had thought it would cost more!'

echo round the room and I look at the nurse, knowing deep down that nothing can be done. She shrugs her shoulders (heartless bitch) and I realise we have snatched defeat from the jaws (ha!) of financial victory.

In hospitals everybody is an employee. In dental practice the surgeon is an employer with the rest of the team essentially a replaceable chorus or corps of employees. Although replaceable, for smooth efficient running, it is best that the team be held together in a stable manner. This inevitably means a large degree of biting one's tongue at staff incompetence and inactivity. A happy relationship with staff means that the important variable, the patients, can be treated by a team who work happily and efficiently together with one common goal – payment of my ridiculously large tax bill.

We seem to have strayed once again from the core subject of ballet in the desire to relate THE INTERESTING THINGS. However, the reader who has reached this far would be surprised if it were CB rather than JB who had the (dental) last word. 'Imbrication' – now there is a word to impress those who have not had the benefit of reading this book. It comes from the Latin for roof tiles and refers to the overlapping of teeth. But perhaps you already knew that. I thought not. Worry not, following your astute purchase of this book you will never be at a loss for words if you find yourself having to talk to a dentist – or roof tiler.... The two are unlikely to be confused – unlike barrister and barista. The difference here, of course, is that barristers earn considerably more.

Self-Assessment Exercise

When JB was a Junior Mixed Infant, classes at school consisted of one teacher and forty or so children sat in rows rather like a cinema with a large blackboard taking the place of the screen. We were in desks for two, with the writing surface lifting up like a lid – inside we kept our pencils, crayons and all the other paraphernalia needed by children when they were not busy chanting their multiplication tables or being beaten. In those days there were no calculators and we also had to learn to read, as there was no round the clock television. All that has changed dramatically and such old-fashioned skills are no longer thought necessary. We now have 'role play', and to show that this book has fully embraced modern life, teaching methods and the like, the reader is now offered a self-assessment exercise. This will prove that knowledge has been imparted and retained and that the reader is now fully equipped to participate in a wide range of dance situations. It is a test, but remember, there is no failure, no losers – only winners. By just reading so far you have become a more rounded, self-aware, fulfilled and dynamic person. Doubly so if you have bought two copies of the book! Remember, if less is more, then more must be even much more. Think about it.

The Texan oil baron

You are Educational Officer for a ballet in Texas (we know it sounds bizarre, but work with us). An oil magnate engages you in conversation as to whether a production might be staged at his ranch.

Of course I want it big! Do I look like the kinda guy who does things small? I want everything big – big stage, big production, big girls. I wanna let those losers at the Dallas Cowboys know how a show is put on. What are we talking here? I want big blonde girls. Dolly Parton but taller. Much taller. Just as soon as the ice cream waterfall is switched off, the lights dim and the helicopter comes in with the stage hanging underneath. The girls are doing that number from *Swan Lake,* you know, the one with the fancy footwork, real complicated – you know that? But big.

Your answer:

1. Big? I've seen bigger high school productions. Let me speak with my associate from Las Vegas.
2. The minimum dimensions for a stage are…
3. You know your own mind, but have these bums from Dallas been keeping you out of the loop? Have your people talk to my people at Friends of the Ballet. For a few million we can get you the biggest corporate sponsorship deal imaginable. Why, if money is no object we might even get your name woven into those towels the girls rub themselves down with between shows!

The support group

You are invited to a support group where, after the initial introductions, the first delegate announces:

> Hello, I am Z (not his real name)

He is greeted, 'Welcome Z, Hi Z ' and there is a short pause for general hugging, then he continues:

> I went to a ballet and was amazed to find that one of dancers seemed obsessed with me. She seemed to stare right at me, looking deep into my eyes. She seemed to penetrate deep into my very soul. I am confused. Should I make a move before the company moves on? Should I get myself, or her, or the theatre exorcised? Should I continue to wear that new cardigan my mother knitted for me if it has that effect on women?

Your answer:

1. Ballerinas are often members of white witch covens. She was indeed looking into your soul, but as you have had no ill effects, she was probably satisfied. You can protect yourself in the future by making regular large payments to Friends of the Ballet.

2. She was 'spotting' – holding her sight onto a far object (and you were sat in the cheapest seats at the back) – so that when spinning she would not lose her balance.

3. There is a new aftershave on the market which does have this effect on women – it smells of money. It is not known whether a hand-knitted cardigan has similar properties but the costume department of the Victoria and Albert Museum may be able to help you.

The cocktail party

You are a socialite invited to a cocktail party and overhear mothers speaking competitively about their children (is there any other way parents do speak about their offspring? We think not.) Your challenge is to join in with some suitable remark. The conversation goes something along the lines of:

Gruyere is so keen on her dancing class and she is doing so well. We think she is going to be advanced to the next class very soon.

That is so nice – it will be company for Camembert who has already been accelerated, but she may not stay there very long. We hear she might be going into a special stream for the super-able.

Well, Wensleydale is of course doing marvellously, but she is growing so tall that we think she might have to become a supermodel instead. She will be far too tall just to be a ballerina.

Your answer:

1. She must borrow our French au pair, learn French and become a Bluebell Girl at the Paris Lido.
2. The average height for a ballerina is 5 foot 4 inches / 163 cm – so that when she stands on her pointe slippers and the man is behind her, her head will come just under his eyeline.
3. Our chalet maid's boyfriend's former lover is an orthopaedic surgeon – he specialises in removing the growth centres from the limbs and preventing untoward height gain.

Remember, there are no wrong answers and everybody is a winner!

Glossary

It should be noted that in these days of the internet, which can be readily accessed with a smartphone (or in airline parlance, 'hand-held portable electronic device'), this is not an exhaustive list of ballet terms, or anything else for that matter. It is just a list of interesting words which might prove useful – after reading this book new social circles may well be now experienced! So do not be surprised when you find the first entry is a decadent drink of French origin famous in artistic circles, then banned, then re-invented. As stated, you are now a different person and will be moving in different circles and talking about different things. Thanks to this book.

Absinthe
Known in the 19th century as the Green Goddess, this drink acquired such a bad reputation it was banned. A distillation of wine and herbs including the herb wormwood (Latin absinthium) forms a clear extract which turns a milky greenish yellow when water is added. It is drunk by dripping it through a perforated spoon containing a lump of sugar. Modern imitations have been developed which leave out the dangerous wormwood.

Allongé
From the French 'lengthened' and designating an elongated line, usually between the forward and backward stretched arms. It can also be used in the term café allongé (weaker but larger than an espresso) – further information about the whole coffee question will be found in the section specially dedicated to coffee.

Aplomb
Fr. balance. The head and small of the back are in a straight line held directly above the supporting foot.

Arabesque
One leg is lifted behind with a straight knee; it is the 'classical' ballerina pose.

Avant, En
Fr. forward. This designates all movements which are directed in a forward direction.

Balancé
Fr. balance. A rocking step foot to foot.

Ballon
Fr. balloon. When a dancer seems to pause in mid-air during a jump.

Barre
The wooden bar on the walls of the dance studio.

Battlement
Fr. beating. This is the beating movement of the leg.

Beards
How many male dancers have beards? There are no official statistics available but JB did not think he had even seen so much as a moustache up to the writing of this – and then suddenly, there it was – a beard. This was at Independent Ballet Wales' production of *The Bride of Flowers*. The British Medical Journal once ran a paper correlating different professions and callings with facial hair – maximum in the Armed Forces (where a moustache was compulsory during the First World War) and minimum in the clergy. As an aside, the Victorians considered that kissing a man without a moustache was like eating egg without salt.

Benesh
The Benesh notation represents the most widely used international system of dance notation. Similar to musical notation, the positions and movements of the body are written onto five lines.

Boredom
It is to be sincerely hoped that the possessor of this book will never suffer from this, but it is reported that a painter who had to paint maple leaves on a backcloth got fed up of the task – a solitary oak leaf appears alone amongst them.

Cakewalk
This word has been adopted into current language as symbolic of something easily achieved, but its origin has quite the opposite meaning. It derives from dances by plantation slaves in the Southern United States who would ridicule by mimicry and exaggeration the dance and walking styles of their masters. High stepping and overblown gestures were used as dancers rivalled each other in achieving the most flamboyant style, with the winners awarded a cake. It was danced to ragtime music.

Cabriole
Fr. from Italian capriola, leap of a goat. A leaping step where the stretched legs are beaten in the air.

Cambré
Fr. curved. The bending of the body from the waist.

Champagne.
That famous expensive German drink. Well, expensive it certainly is – due to two reasons. Firstly, it is fermented a second time (the second being in the bottle), but primarily because it is strictly controlled – Appellation d'Origine Contrôleé. In the Treaty of Versailles of 1919 the famous 'Champagnerparagraph' allowed the French to forbid Germans from calling their sparkling wine champagne. So why did JB start by calling this a German drink? Well, bizarrely enough, it follows on from his studying this in Paris. Americans: Paris, France not Paris, Texas. In the history of champagne the Germans play a very important role. At the end of the 18th century young Germans emigrated to the Champagne region of France to make a career, bringing their talent, sense of

commerce and various other skills. They came to dominate it so much that the American consul Robert Tomes wrote in 1867 that there was effectively no champagne house which was not more or less controlled by a German! Florenz-Ludwig Heidsieck founded the first in 1777, followed by the three brothers Mumm, Johann-Joseph Krug, Joseph Jacob Bollinger, Johann Carl Phillip Koch, William Deutz, etc. When they could not set up their own mark they often married the daughter of a French house. By the way, the French do not refer to the abbreviated Moët et Chandon as 'Mo-ay' but 'Moette', as the 't' is elided with the 'e' of et. You probably knew that, but be cautious in advertising this knowledge, especially when others are paying. Which is of course the best way of drinking champagne.

Chassé
Fr. hunted. A sliding step where one foot seems to hunt the other.

Coryphée
A rank of dancer which tends to be falling into disuse but still can occasionally be seen in the dancer lists in some companies.

Cou-de-pied
One foot is placed on the ankle of the other.

Csárdás
This is a dance of Hungarian origin with no specific steps but comprising two parts: slow and melancholy followed by rapid turning and leaping. It can be found in *Coppélia, Raymonda* and the ballroom act of *Swan Lake*.

Dedans
Fr. inside – the inward turning of the arms or legs (en dedans) as opposed to en dehors (outside).

Dégagé
Fr. disengaged – the shifting of weight from one foot to the other.

Entrechat
This is a criss-crossing of the legs while the dancer is in the air – each crossing is counted as two movements. Wayne Sleep (yes, he was the one who became a principal dancer with The Royal Ballet at 5′2′, the shortest male dancer ever admitted) set a world record by doing an entrechat douze – a jump with six beats. This was in 1973 and the record still stands. An entrechat deux can be called a Royale after Louis X1V who was unable to perform a quatre.

Entrée
An appetiser or starter before the main course – see the menu at the restaurant Musée d'Orsay where there are French and English versions. It is NOT THE MAIN COURSE.

Extension
Forget hair or house-building connotations, this refers in ballet to the capability of a dancer to raise and hold the extended leg in the air.

Female athletic triad
A syndrome comprising menstrual dysfunction (usually amenorrhea) with low bone mass and energy deficit.

FRAD
Fellow of the Royal Academy of Dance.

Freed
(of London). The famous ballet supply shop conveniently located near the Royal Opera House.

French manicure
The famous 'two-tone' technique was in fact invented in 1974 by a Hollywood make-up artist, Jeff Pink. He had noticed how Parisian models rubbed white pencil beneath their unpolished nail tips for a 'clean natural' look.

G String

One of the strings on a violin – don't worry which. If you need to know, then you will know.

Grand écart

Écarté means wide apart in French so this term is the formal description for what is more colloquially known as 'the splits'.

Glissade

A gliding step between larger steps.

Heimlich manoeuvre

A manoeuvre designed to dislodge impacted food and a technique which should be learnt by all – and despite its comprehensive nature, not from a book such as this!

Jeté

This comes from the French jeter (to throw) but actually means any jump which moves from one foot to another. Thus it can be a jump forwards, backwards, in a single direction or turning. It can be a jump to the side (as in Rocky Horror!).

Léotard

This was the invention of a French trapeze artist, Jules Léotard (1830-1870). It is a one-piece all over suit, equally beloved by acrobats.

Musée d'Orsay

The Orsay railway station and hotel were built between September 1898 and July 1900 on the ruins of the Cour des Comptes which had been burnt by the Commune in 1871. Just look carefully at those dates – less than two years! But there were no computers to screw things up on a massive scale and no breaks for double skinny decaff lattes. The station continued to function as such until 1959 but the hotel did not close until 1973. The museum was finally opened in December 1986 and is a far, far better building than most of those museums in 'purpose built accommodation' –

i.e. concrete which stains and cracks, and where you cannot find the front door!

Otolaryngologist
More usually known as ear, nose and throat (ENT) surgeons, these are the cream of the surgical world and with their mastery of refined delicate operations have the reputation of being superb lovers.

Pas
This is the general term for a step – and is the word for all steps in ballet. It may be qualified to explain the nature e.g. pas de chat where the step is likened to that of a cat, or to indicate the number of dancers e.g. pas de deux, de trois, de quatre (two, three, four).

Pas de bourrée
Running tiptoe on the spot.

Pirouette
Fr. spinning top. In ballet this designates one or more turns of the body on one leg.

Political correctness
The word 'handicap' has been removed from tribunals 'because it has a negative connotation'. The thing is, there are not many beneficial handicaps which we can celebrate. The reader is invited to send in any examples if there are some overlooked by this book – they will be forwarded to the relevant authorities.

Prolegomenon
A preliminary discussion at the beginning of a book. Every book written by JB and his colleague and sometime co-author John Riddington Young has one. It seems mean to deprive the reader. It is not to be confused with a foreword, which is written by a different person and precedes the author's preface (which is an introduction to a book). Beware of falling into the trap of muddling this with a prologue, which is an opening to a story

that establishes the setting. This term was used extensively by Frankie Howerd in the comedy series *Up Pompeii*.

ROH
The Royal Opera House, London. It should be noted that the world still has other monarchies, many of which are equipped with opera houses.

Renversé
Fr. overturned. This is the bending of the body while turning in time, which naturally disturbs normal balance.

As might be expected, there is also a café renversé. Of Swiss origin (allegedly), this starts with milk as the base (just over half the volume) and then coffee is added. Will it ever end? Probably not.

Ronde de jambe
Fr. circle of the leg. Unsurprisingly, this designates circular movements of the leg, either on the ground or in the air. The astute reader will by now be realising that a French reader has quite an advantage with these terms.

Rosin
A sticky substance made from thc sap of fir trees which is crushed into a powder to prevent ballet shoes from slipping.

Saut
Fr. leap. A jump off both feet landing in the same position.

Spotting
The technique whereby a dancer visually fixes onto a distant object whilst spinning to avoid dizziness. Try it for yourself when next on a fairground roundabout, or when very drunk.

Soutenu
Fr. sustained. In ballet this designates a s…….d movement. Did you get it right?

Turn-out
This is the turn-out of the leg from the hip to a right angle and is the first principle of the academic style upon which all ballet steps depend. The observant may recognise someone who has had ballet training by the subconscious adoption of this position occasionally.

Vaseline
Applied to the hair to reflect the light and make it look shiny – Robert Helpmann's make-up trick, learnt in Australia.

Yaffinalarf
The correct response on being told the price of a programme at the ROH.

The Adult Section

Including:

- **A Walk on the Wild Side**
- **A Philistine's Guide to the Arts**
- **The coffee question**

A Walk on the Wild Side

There will be readers who will find the following to be neither interesting nor helpful, but despite this, it is included. Part of the reason for this has been the encouragement of two famous dancers, La Goulue and Josephine Baker, neither of whom eschewed the racier side of life. Their sage advice cannot be quoted directly as it was revealed to JB in a dream. Anyway, it is to be hoped that the title *The Adult Section* will be warning enough to the sensitive – rather like the helpful little warnings found ever more frequently before the start of a television programme.

In the state of California (USA), striptease dancers, once undressed, may only come to within a certain distance from the edge of the stage. The rules against public indecency are written in such a way that a dancer may undress to her thong – but must wear tights underneath. In contrast, the state of Texas allows fully licensed dancers to have a certain degree of freedom, though local ordinances may interpret things differently. A licensed dancer can be identified as such because she will have an identity card with photograph fastened to her ankle. This is a useful piece of information gladly imparted to any reader who might be embarrassed to pose the question. In England, it is not normally regarded as proper to ask someone from which county they originate. If he is a Yorkshireman, he will undoubtedly have already told you so. If he isn't, then why embarrass the poor fellow?

A dancer who is not professionally registered (we are not talking about ballet dancers here) may be SOB graded – sex orientated business, and this is where the attention to detail really does come into force. One only wonders if whoever dreamt this up had an eye to creating 'interesting' jobs for himself and his fellow inspectors. These girls are allowed to dance topless, but their breasts must be covered with a latex paint in a triangle to include the nipple. This is best applied in a thick layer – so that it can be easily removed, peeling off in a single piece. SOB licensed dancers are not allowed G strings but have to wear a more substantial lower garment. This usually means that she will wear a garter belt for appreciative members of the public to fold dollar bills. Of course in the USA (possibly uniquely among countries?) all paper money is the same size no matter what the denomination. In other words, $100 is the same size as $1 – so be careful!

A dancer will usually choose which songs she will dance to and as her dance will last the length of the piece, then unusually long ones such as The Moody Blues' *Knights in White Satin* or Queen's *Bohemian Rhapsody* are rarely heard in lap dancing clubs. A dancer of generous spirit may, however, start her routine during the break song – the music sometimes played as a sort of interval when there is nobody on stage. This might be expressed as 'I'll fit you up' – a Cajun expression to be found in New Orleans and conveys the meaning that as a favour I'll give you something extra – i.e. more time than the length of a usual song. The reader should not fail to notice the diligence which has gone into unearthing these details.

Much vital research was undertaken by one of the contributors (we will not specify which) amongst Parisian nightclubs. Dancers there have a similar life-span to that found in ballet. For French cabaret performers the ceiling seems to be about 35 – after that they allegedly look too old – according to the dancers themselves. They might also run out of steam. Dancing can use up 400 calories per hour – but a hectic routine might use up 600. That is why they are thin. Cabaret dancers can work six to seven days a week with up to two performances a day. Nobody can drop out, especially in the smaller troupes – sickness is just not allowed! The majority started off with ballet training – which is the basis for most dance routines. Ballet is usually the grounding not only for cabaret dancers but also folk. In Soviet times those who on graduation from ballet school did not achieve a position in a ballet group had to dance as Cossacks, etc. Those with any knowledge of the subject will realise that Cossacks have very specific facial features, which are often lacking in so-called Cossack troupes.

The astute reader will perhaps wonder why this section seems to be confined to foreign shores. The answer is simple – it is at academic conferences and the like where JB is invited to give presentations, etc. and can hardly refuse the generous (and sometimes unusual) hospitality shown by his hosts. But before we jump to the erroneous conclusion that the arts in Britain are constrained by a puritanical grip, consider the following. It has been reported (*Daily Mail* 6 Feb 2022) that an event at the Institute of Contemporary Arts (ICA) was to feature 13 artists, including sex workers, a porn actress and strippers, alongside art featuring sex, nudity and violence. Accounts for the ICA, based on The Mall in London, showed that it received £2.7 million in five Government grants the previous year. During the Covid pandemic it was awarded £789,000 from the Culture Recovery Fund and two of its executives are paid more than £100,000 a year.

A Philistine's Guide to the Arts

The way to approach a masterpiece is in silence – so that it can speak to you. JB has managed to mix in circles far above his social or academic position by using such simple ploys. Similarly, on being questioned as to an opinion on wine – the sort of thing wine snobs are continually pestering those who simply want to enjoy a drink, the company and the ambience. They want to show off their (probably newly acquired at a course) knowledge. The only response is:

'Drunk from a glass like this – how could I possibly tell?'

Then make a beeline for the nearest attractive woman and avoid the bore for the rest of the evening. As an added bonus there now follows a short piece about things to say when tongue-tied at an 'Arts' event.

On seeing an asymmetrical piece of sculpture:

'I had the same problem with IKEA
Will they manage to get it repaired?'

'I did a course on this painter – he died in poverty yet his sister had sex just once with just one of his drinking buddies and the son from that union inherited millions!'

On seeing a collection of modern painting:

'How old were the children who did these?'

The painter clearly has astigmatism – just look at the foreground through your spectacles held at arm's length then slowly rotate them (this usually works if done with confidence – sometimes you need to sneak back to see others surreptitiously trying it and explaining it to others; what fun!).

'Do you know the prints of this are outsold only by the half-naked green lady standing in a pond / the girl serving at tennis / those puppies playing a game of poker?'

On meeting a vegetarian (found more often in the Arts world, wearing black and looking rather pale):

'Well then, what is the capital of Vegetaria?'

On seeing a weird still life:

'What do you think it might have looked like if the artist had been able to finish it?'

Become obsessed with the attendant's chair or a fire extinguisher.

I prefer the original!

At a ballet performance:

'When does the singing start?'

'My therapy group is looking into starting this.'

'The best of these ballet stars – you know, the really good ones, get to audition for Vegas. Of course, they all have to have implants.

Of course to progress to the very top, most ballerinas have their outer toes surgically removed.'

The coffee question

JB goes off on a rant. The contributors beg the indulgence of the reader once again whilst JB gets something off his chest. It may even strike a chord. Why is it that it is so difficult to order a cup of coffee in Britain now? In Germany 'eine Milchkaffee' is perfectly well understood, in France 'un crème' brings the same result. Yet, despite using his mother tongue in England, JB has great difficulty. Everything seems to have gone quasi Italian, and the waitress (who usually speaks neither English nor Italian) seems never to have heard of coffee made with milk. What tends to happen is that after much tutting and eyes raised to the ceiling, a cup of strong black coffee is proffered with a tiny plastic tub of some form of white milk product at the side, or a glass too hot to hold containing coffee which probably has cocoa sprinkled on the top. We are informed that the coffee is espresso (most people say expresso), that it is Italian (in the sort of manner that implies coffee was either invented or grows there) and there is the definite implication that we are ignoramuses. In reality, espresso is .... well, the short definition of espresso is 'very strong coffee'. But espresso is much too fascinating to be described in such a fashion. And the art of creating espresso is too seductive to not include all its aspects. And why is this? And why are we stating this? Well, we are lucky to have a contribution from an expert in the culinary arts who has written on the subject especially for this book. It has to be put in the Adult Section, as seduction is not a subject we can safely leave to the general readership. This is particularly so as Donna is, herself, an extremely attractive and seductive person. JB used to travel miles to the coffee shop in which she worked, in a tiny place called Cobden, which, for those of you who remember, is rather like the television programme *Petticoat Junction*. Ah, memories.

But before Donna is allowed her piece it is fitting that a little historical background is inserted – the reader would expect nothing less. Coffee brewing was in fact a haphazard affair until the late 19th century when the invention of the percolation method brought some regularity to its taste. However, it was not until the 1930s that the first modern espresso maker was created. This was designed by Francesco Illy (father of Ernesto) and used compressed air instead of steam to create the required pressure. It was the son, Ernesto (1925-2008) who helped introduce espresso to the world and whose family name is synonymous in Italy with this. According to his obituary (*The Times* 26 February 2008) he regarded the *Starbucks* chain with admiration, not for the standard of its coffee – Americans, he felt, always confused quality with quantity – but because it had brought new customers to coffee who might one day go on to discover real espresso. Illy's company is also a prominent supporter of contemporary art and has commissioned Jeff Koons, among others, to design its cups. Funnily enough, he himself began his mornings with a large cup of India tea! Another useful fact to know is that although the company sells coffee to 140 countries, in Italy itself less elite brands such as Lavazza still dominate the domestic and bar market.

Donna will now explain in her own words:

> Espresso is crafted by a barista (or coffee wench, if you happen to be in Cobden) and the well-made espresso is sweet and smooth and aromatic. Begin with freshly roasted coffee beans. The ideal roast for espresso is light to preserve the aroma and sugars. Most people believe the bean should be roasted very dark for an espresso…they are mistaken. The freshly and lightly roasted coffee beans are ground to nearly a powder. Assuming the espresso is to be made with a machine, the ground coffee is spooned into a portafilter. Here comes the fun, and most important part. The coffee is pressed with a tamper under 5 pounds of pressure. The portafilter is then tapped to release any coffee clinging to its sides. It is then re-tamped under 30 pounds of pressure and then a shiny surface is created by twisting the tamper. So, let us go through this 'dance' again…. spoon, tamp, tap, tamp and twist. The resulting product is called a 'puck'. The puck-packed portafilter is inserted into the espresso machine where hot water is forced through the puck of coffee. As stated earlier, packing the coffee is the most important part of espresso making as it is essential for even extraction. After a 25 to 30 second 'draw' the finished product is a shot (1.5 ounces / 440 ml) of espresso resembling dark, warmed honey. The ultimate prize in the perfect shot of espresso, however, is the crema. The crema is the layer of rich, dark, reddish brown foam covering the surface.

Ohhh…the seduction. The sweet smooth aroma of the beans, the tamp, tap, tamp and twist dance of puck creation and the climax of a sweet, rich, warmed honey espresso covered with foamy crema. Ahhhhh….

How's that? Doesn't it make you want to immediately go out for an espresso? Or take a cold shower?

JB asks for a milky coffee and gets some boiling liquid in a glass without a handle which is too hot to touch, and which is covered in cocoa. What is worse, if he is less than delighted the implication is that he asked for the wrong thing, or is too stupid to understand the new descriptive terms which the fashionable have introduced for coffee. Espresso is, in his opinion, one method of making coffee – the steam pressure, etc. It comes out incredibly strong. Another is by using a filter paper. Then there is the cafetière which seems to have been introduced into Britain about a decade ago and which is only being discovered now in Germany (where it is called Kaffeedruckmaschine – 'Druck' meaning pressure).

For those of our readers who are unsure as to how things are currently organised, then the following may be of help:

Caffè latte – this comes in a glass too hot to hold

Caffè espresso – this blows your head off

Caffè Americano – the name tends to put you off but we are reliably informed it contains no ketchup or chewing gum!

Café allongé (from the French 'outspread' – yes, this does sound familiar – it is touched upon in the glossary) is a drink midway in strength between an espresso and Americano. It can also be called espresso lungo, but not by JB!

Café renversé – now where have I read that before?

Other choices: (remember now the ground-breaking experimental nature of this book which allows interactive participation – as the months go by there are bound to be new terms devised.)

....

....

....

This was just about ready for final reading when Donna (bless her) came up with even more information which complicates matters further. We have, by now, got to grips with the fact that an espresso with steamed milk is 'Milchkaffee', aka latte.

But, if steamed cream (although most American coffeehouses use a strange liquid called Half & Half) is added to the shot of espresso it is called a *breve*. In other words, it is a coffee drunk in a glass too hot to hold and with the added bonus of adding extra girth!

If the milk in the latte is steamed and foamed it is called a *cappuccino* – apparently so named because when introduced in Italy it was named after the Capucin friars, as the colour resembled that of their robes.

But that is not all. We can kick the cappuccino up one notch by adding chocolate syrup and topping it with whipped cream and calling it a *café mocha*. Typically the whipped cream is sprayed out of a can onto the top of the café mocha and then topped with chocolate sprinkles called 'jimmies', or a dusting of cocoa. We now go on a little excursion into the realms of weirdness but, true to our motto of giving you 'The Interesting Stuff', we cannot allow prejudice, squeamishness, or even taste to restrain us. Donna recommends whipped cream-in-a-can as it has a nice consistency and is not too sweet. She baulks, however, at the frozen plastic in a plastic bowl…cool whip. Amongst other 'qualities' it possesses, one which worries her is that it never changes temperature (among other things). Cool whip feels the same temperature on the tongue frozen as it does at room temperature. There must be a market for it, but we advise against using it. We similarly advise strongly against the following, and for this reason it is found in the removable adult section. Once again, we quote Donna directly (but sadly mere print cannot, of course, reproduce her melodic lilting accent):

An advantage of using the spray-in-a-can whipped cream is that when the product is gone there may be a bit of propellant left to 'huff'. We actually had an employee, an adult employee, who saved the cans when they were empty, put them on top of the espresso machine (better huffing when warmed?) and inhaled the leftover propellant for a buzz. Weird.

Donna is of course an American, and cheerfully puts up with the gentle barbs found scattered throughout the book. She even goes so far as to add one herself. What a girl! Or should we say 'Whadda gal!'

As long as we are on the topic of spray-in-a-can foods, it's not ketchup or chewing gum that would (or would not) make a café Americano…it is *Easy cheese.* Aerosol cheese.

This is cheese (or perhaps what is sometimes euphemistically – perhaps for legal reasons – known as cheese-like substitute) which comes in an aerosol can. When the cap is activated it shoots out a yellow (but a type of yellow not found in nature – it actually appears fluorescent!) substance which JB can only liken to something seen in a rhinology clinic. It is squirted on the top of shepherds' pie chicken, hamburgers – you name it, there is probably somebody somewhere who has 'enhanced' a dish with aerosol cheese. While we are about it, have you noticed that the Americans are happy to use aerosol AERO but insist on airplane for aeroplane? Still, like the wayward teenagers in a family, we know we won't understand them, they sometimes drive us mad, but we love them all the same. Well, Donna anyway.

So there we have it, a short tutorial on coffee. In France, the above may be found, but JB always asks for un crème (note that it is masculine 'un' as it is short for café crème and café is masculine – equally when asking for a table for one, always say une personne even when the person is a man; personne is always feminine). In Germany, you already know to ask for Milchkaffee. In Britain stick to tea if you don't want to memorise and try to pronounce all these Italian terms.

Why have the Italians got this seeming monopoly on coffee? No coffee is actually grown there. It is the same with Belgians and chocolate. People might think that the English were not well-versed in either. They would be wrong. Britain has the highest chocolate consumption in Europe – a KitKat bar is eaten every 46 seconds (not by the same person) and firms such as Cadbury, Rowntree, Fry and Mackintosh are known, and export, worldwide. Dr Johnson did his writing in a London coffee house. In 1750 there were more than 2,000 (yes, that is two thousand!) coffee houses in the capital. And Garibaldi? We think not. He didn't even invent the biscuits. But this is beginning to turn into a rant…

But as the subject of chocolate has come up, recent research has shown that increasing some things might not always be to the good. We think 60% cocoa content tastes better than 75%. Thanks must go to the late Mr Richard Hinds for drawing the attention of JB to the fact that the 100% Bourbon which has been developed is no improvement on the 80% – we both considered that Pamela Anderson fell into the same trap.